John Clarke (29 July 1948 – 9 April 2017) was a writer and performer who provided the following account of his activities:

CLARKE, John, Dip Lid, PhD in Cattle (Oxen). Advisor and comforter to various governments. Born 1948. Educ. subsequently. Travelled extensively throughout Holy Lands, then left New Zealand for Europe. Stationed in London 1971–73. Escaped (Decorated). Rejoined unit. Arrived Australia 1977. Held positions with ABC Radio (Sckd), ABC Television (Dfnct), Various Newspapers (Dcd), and Aust. Film Industry (Fkd). Went on to become a freelance expert specialising in matters of a general character. Recreations: Whistling.

mrjohnclarke.com

DAWE, Bryan. Born in Port Adelaide. Escaped high school at fifteen. Lived in London. Returned 1972. For four years Senior Executive for Lunch & Dinner assisting Astor Records. Retired hurt, travelled, and wrote songs for next ten years. Minor hit, with musician Steve Groves— winner, Australian Song Festival 1976. Wrote for ABC Radio while head of Radio Comedy Unit for four years. Performed characters Roly Parks and Sir Murray Rivers QC for the past twenty-eight years.

Met Mr Clarke Esq. 1987. Spent next thirty years with aforementioned gentleman trying to get the powerful to put their hands up on the table where we could see them. Traveller to Middle East, visual artist. Exhibition 'Tangier Illusions' shown in Tangier, Morocco and Bendigo 2017.

bryandawe.com

Also by John Clarke

Still the Two

A Dagg at My Table

The Tournament

The Howard Miracle

The 7.56 Report

The Even More Complete Book of Australian Verse

The Catastrophe Continues

Tinkering

John Clarke

A pleasure to be here

The best of Clarke & Dawe 1989–2017

Introduced by Bryan Dawe

TEXT PUBLISHING MELBOURNE AUSTRALIA

textpublishing.com.au

The Text Publishing Company
Swann House
22 William Street
Melbourne Victoria 3000
Australia

Published in 2017 by The Text Publishing Company
Reprinted 2017, 2018

Book design by Text
Cover photos by Stewart Thorn
Typeset by J&M Typesetting

Printed and bound in Australia by Griffin Press, an accredited ISO/NZS 1401:2004 Environmental Management System printer

National Library of Australia Cataloguing-in-Publication entry:
Creator: Clarke, John (1948–2017), author.
Title: A pleasure to be here (the best of Clarke and Dawe 1989–2017) / by John Clarke.
ISBN: 9781925603200 (paperback)
ISBN: 9781925626254 (ebook)
Subjects: Current affair (Australia). 7.30 report (Television program). Political satire, Australian. Politicians—Australia—Caricatures and cartoons. Australia—Politics and government—Humour.

Contents

The Story of *Clarke & Dawe*

by Bryan Dawe

Mr Clarke Esq. and I met during 1987 when I had just been appointed the first head of the ABC Radio Comedy Unit in Melbourne. In addition to writing and producing my own work, my role entailed garnering writers and performers to create comedy. My first instinct was to approach John Clarke, who had been unceremoniously booted off ABC Radio by a far-sighted genius from the ABC Talent Eradication Unit (NSW division) a number of years earlier, for being 'too political'.

I had never met John but loved his Fred Dagg monologues and thought his writing and performances for *The Gillies Report*, particularly his Farnarkeling segment, were sheer satirical genius—not a joke within cooee and delivered with a straight-faced seriousness that perfectly mirrored the most earnest of sports commentators.

Asked what I expected him to do, I advised John he had free rein. We recorded some Fred Dagg pieces and then, at the end of the third week, he suggested recording one of several interviews he had recently written for a newspaper.

The first interview we did together was John as Prince Charles. His Royal Highness (as John insisted he be called) explained that he was in Australia to deliver a replica of the barge that transported food out to Captain Cook's *Endeavour* in Portsmouth. It ran for five and a half minutes and included HRH admitting that he adored the Goons and could imitate Eccles's voice for hours at a time in the bath.

We had been doing the interviews on ABC radio for a year or so when John rang one morning and asked, 'Want to try these interviews for television?'

'Sure,' I said, assuming it was something we would discuss in detail some time in the future.

'What are you doing this afternoon?' he said.

'Nothing much,' I replied.

'I'll pick you up at one.'

Channel Nine wanted John to do a Fred Dagg monologue at the end of *A Current Affair* each Friday, but Mr Clarke had other ideas and talked them into letting us record three interviews.

So with the words, 'Let's go and stick some ferrets down some trousers,' we duly headed off to Channel Nine. I think you can over-prepare for a thirty-year career collaborating on radio and television.

John got the Dagg monologues out the way and then we hopped into the interviews. The tapes were sent up to Sydney that same afternoon. Jana Wendt, the *ACA* host, loved them and, at 6.55 p.m. that evening, the first television segment of what would become *Clarke & Dawe* went to air. Jana left *ACA* in 1992, but we enjoyed a seven-year run, until in 1996 we were advised that our satirical services on the program were no longer required.

So, a short break and back to Auntie we went, this time to television.

Two fundamentals of any collaboration, if it is to survive, are trust and respect. John and I had that for each other, in spades.

John's visceral loathing of pomposity, and his talent for distilling hours of political bluster into a two-and-a-half-minute kernel of truth, ensured that being handed a script by him each week and invited to address it was like becoming a kid shredding Christmas gift paper.

In the early, pre-internet days, John would fax drafts of the weekly scripts to me, we'd run them through over the phone, and then the diamond polisher would go back to work. The term 'final draft' was an oxymoron. A shared love of ad-libbing meant the script was never finished until we'd recorded, and it had been edited for broadcast. After a while, we rarely bothered with rehearsal. We'd meet at the ABC studios around 2.30 p.m., John with three or four different scripts in hand, we'd frock up, run through the scripts, then the hem would be shortened or lengthened and the style of the frock adjusted, if necessary, during a take.

We always tried to record more than one script, keeping the reserve tank topped up lest one of us tripped over the furniture or couldn't play the next week. We never missed a segment of *Clarke & Dawe* during the entire journey.

Possibly the most frequent question asked of me over the years was 'How do you keep a straight face during the interviews?' The secret was to never look at John's eyes, but to focus instead on his forehead. To look into John's mischievous eyes as he deadpanned responses was to invite paroxysms of laughter.

No one could make me laugh like John Clarke could. No one ever will again.

John and I were both blessed and honoured to have had a loyal audience who allowed the creature *Clarke & Dawe* to keep breathing for thirty years. For that, we thank you.

It remained, to its end, as much fun to perform each week together as is allowable under the Geneva Convention. In a sense it was easy. As the great American satirist Will Rogers observed, 'There's no trick to being a humorist when you have the whole government working for you.'

It was a very long innings and John Clarke carried his bat.

The Hawke Ascendancy

11 March 1983 – 20 December 1991

Mr Hawke, is it true that interest rates will go up to seventeen per cent?
I was unfaithful to my wife, yes.

Were you unfaithful to the electorate?
No, I was not unfaithful to the electorate.

Mr Hawke, why did you spend last week on national television talking about your penis?
Talking about my penis?

Yes, your penis.
I didn't talk about my penis last week on national television. What are you talking about?

Why do you get so emotional about Australia?
I love Australia. I think it's far and away the best…
Look, I was having a wee the other night, and I just happened to look down, and I thought, 'What a marvellous, fantastic country this is.'

The Hon. Paul Keating
Treasurer of Australia

It's entirely my fault.

Mr Keating, thanks for your time.
A pleasure. Have some brie.

Can I ask if you've seen the recent figures?
The cost of living figures?

Yes.
Yes, they're very distressing, aren't they?

You're not happy with them?
It's beginning to look as if we've made some very big mistakes. We've taken policy positions on interest rates, deregulation of the currency market and so on and, as I say, it looks as if we were wrong.

Are you saying it's not working?
It's a complete cock-up.

How did the government misread things so badly?
It wasn't the government; it was me. I had a pretty good run for a while there but the wheels have come off. She's cactus.

What went wrong?
I'm probably not the person to ask. I haven't known too much about what's been going on since the middle of 1985. Perhaps I should have said so earlier, but when you're the treasurer you can't go about the place telling people to abandon ship. It's been a hell of a thing to live with.

If I can say this without appearing insensitive, that's probably not the issue.
No, you're right. I've got to stop thinking about myself all the time. It must have been bloody terrible for a lot of people out there. How

they've coped, I'll never know. It says a great deal about ordinary Australians, you know, this whole business. You feel helpless—all that trust and not a bloody clue about what you're doing.

If I could take you back now over some of the things the government has done...
Not the government. Let's be completely clear about this. The policies were mine. It's entirely my fault.

Can I ask you about the May Economic Statement?
Shot in the dark.

Didn't come off?
Never looked like it, unfortunately. Although, of course, the real problem last year was the budget itself.

What aspect of it?
All of it. It actually goes back to the 1984 budget. That's where I lost the plot and realised that, if I just let the economy run, I might be able to dress the results up as our policy, analyse things retrospectively and stress our commitment to whatever appeared to be happening.

Is this where the J-curve comes from?
Yes.

What exactly was the J-curve?
I don't recall exactly what it was now. It might have been a reflection of the way reduced domestic demand translated into a control mechanism for lessening indebtedness over time, but don't hold me to that. I'm not sure that's right.

Didn't it have something to do with the money supply?
It may have. I don't know.

Is it possible for the economy to actually change direction, which is what you seem to be suggesting?
Part of the problem is that the economic advisers and analysts have all been trained by the system which has got us into this position. None

of them has any knowledge of how to change it or what to change it to. All we can do is hope to develop a better sort of Elastoplast. The possibility of actual change is nil.

But isn't it needed?
It's needed urgently, yes. No doubt about that. I'm just telling you it isn't going to happen.

What do you think are the main problems at the moment?
Oh Christ, where to start. Interest rates are appalling, people can't afford to buy houses, we're committed to unemployment, we've trimmed public expenditure so much the place doesn't work, and if the Japanese stop investing in Australia for five minutes it's all over.

Why don't you lower interest rates?
We can't afford to; we're pretending to give tax cuts and that's where we're getting the money from.

Why did you make a speech recently blaming people who live in houses with Hills Hoists and so on?
I haven't been well. I seem to recall giving it a bit of a nudge before making those remarks. It's pointless blaming the victims, of course, and I deeply regret any offence I may have given.

Do you have any concern about the type of society you're creating here?
Yes, that's very worrying. A lot of cowboys have got the run of the joint at the moment. If you saw some of the mongrels I have to deal with your hair would stand bolt upright.

How have your colleagues reacted to the news?
By and large, very well. I've had a lot of support—not from everyone, but that's understandable. There were plenty of people who disagreed with me from day one.

Who were they?
Oh, Barry Jones and all those brainy pricks.

But weren't they right?
Yes, but I didn't know that then. I thought I had a dream. I didn't know it was just a lot of ego until it was too late.

What will you do?
I'll stay in the job, because I've told Bob I would, but I don't know how long I can go on pretending.

You feel you've let the country down?
Of course. I've let the country down very badly. Tell the people I am deeply, deeply, deeply sorry.

I will.

The Hon. John Dawkins
Minister for Education

The best way to buy chalk.

Mr Dawkins, thanks for your time.
It's a pleasure.

You're the minister for education, aren't you?
Yes, I am.

How long have you been minister for education?
I've been the minister for about eighteen months or two years.

How did it happen? Do you remember how it first happened?
I started off just being a spokesman, having a few views on education—things like TAFEs and the primary schools, the best way to buy chalk, small things like that.

What is the best way to buy chalk?
You get it in sticks, I suppose you would call them, about four inches long.

How many would you buy at a time?
If you know where to go, I've seen people buying boxes of twenty and thirty at a time.

Could you go out of here now, say, and buy some chalk?
Yes, no trouble.

And what have you done as minister for education?
I've introduced a very full range of reforms right across the entire spectrum of the Australian education system and the curric...cccricc...

The curriculum?
Yes, the curricoleum.

The curriculum.
The what?

The curriculum.
Yes, that too.

What sort of reform?
What I was instructed to do by the prime minister and the treasurer.

Which was what?
Get rid of the poor. I've introduced the tertiary education tax.

What is that?
It's a way of getting university students to pay for the costs involved in university education.

Aren't the universities already paid for?
Yes, they are.

Aren't they funded out of taxation?
Yes, of course they are.

Haven't we already paid them?
Yes, we have.

So you are asking people to pay twice?
Yes.

Will they agree to it?
They won't get into a university if they don't.

Where are you going to get the money from?
The plan is to get it out of them when they've finished their economics degrees.

So, in effect, you're blackmailing them.
Yes.

Who pays their fees in the first place?
They do.

Where do they get the money from?
Probably their parents—I don't know.

Who pays for their accommodation and living expenses and transport and books and so on?
Probably their parents.

And who are you getting into the university system?
At the moment we're getting a lot of people with fairly rich parents.

Is this a good idea?
I think so. They're able to go through university with the same people they went to school with and it helps with carpooling. There's a continuity about it.

Isn't it Labor Party policy to provide free education?
Used to be.

It used to be your policy?
No, we used to be the Labor Party.

If we could turn now to research, which is the other major function of the university system...
That won't change.

How will it be done?
It will be done as it is now.

Where will it be done?
It's a vital function and will continue to be done as it is now, in areas designated for research.

Where?
Oh, Japan, Taiwan, Sweden. They do a lot of it in Europe, America, Spain, Poland, Brazil and Wales.

Do you get out much?
Not anymore, no. I can't. It's too difficult. I've got to put the beard on, the wig, change my suit, jack up the police escort. It's just too hard.

So, what do you do?

I stay at home a lot, watch a bit of television.

Do you read?

Read? No, I don't. Wish I could.

The Hon. Bob Hawke
Prime Minister of Australia

I was unfaithful to my wife.

Mr Hawke, is it true that interest rates will go up to seventeen per cent?
I was unfaithful to my wife, yes.

Mr Hawke, seventeen per cent is appalling. How are people going to cope?
I'm not going to run away from it. It wasn't just my own wife, either. I was unfaithful to a lot of other people's wives, too.

Were you unfaithful to the electorate?
No, I was not unfaithful to the electorate.

What about Mr Punch?
No, I was not unfaithful to Mr Punch. As a matter of fact, I had a couple of words with Mr Punch before the third runway was announced.

What were those couple of words?
I'm not going to tell you what the couple of words were.

Could you tell us what one of the words was?
Well, one of them was 'off'.

And what was the other one?
No. I'm not going to tell you what the other one was.

Mr Hawke, why did you spend last week on national television talking about your penis?
Talking about my penis?

Yes, your penis.
I didn't talk about my penis last week on national television. What are you talking about?

Mr Hawke, with respect, you spoke about your penis on national television on Monday night, Wednesday night, Thursday night, Friday and Saturday nights.
Well, only indirectly, and I didn't mention my penis on Tuesday night on national television. You go and check the facts.

Mr Hawke...
What's your name?

Mr Hawke, with respect, why does the prime minister need to go on national television and, on the one hand, talk about his sexual prowess, and then make some pathetic attempt to woo women voters back by apologising for what he did in the past? What's the problem? Is it psychological?
There is no psychological problem here. Certainly not. None whatsoever.

What's the problem?
Well, I am simply a very sensitive...a very, very sensitive...an extremely sensitive person.

Why do you get so emotional about Australia?
I love Australia. I think it's a fantastic country. I think it's far and away the best...Look, I was having a wee the other night, and I just happened to look down, and I thought, 'What a marvellous, fantastic country this is.' It's just fantastic. It's wonderful. I love it.

You cry a lot, don't you?
I don't think I cry a lot, no.

Mr Hawke, you cried on national television this week. Please.
Oh, I cry on national television, I don't cry in private, but yes, sure, I cry a bit on national television.

Why?
Well, I've seen the trade figures, and I was aware that interest rates were going to seventeen per cent. Anybody would cry. It's tragic. How people are going to cope, I don't know.

You get very emotional about women, too, don't you?
I do get a bit emotional about women.

Why?
I empathise with women. My heart goes out to them. I've got a great deal of sympathy for women.

Why?
They've got no penis.

Mr Hawke, thank you.
Thank you, cock.

The Rt. Hon. Margaret Thatcher
Prime Minister of the United Kingdom

We needed something to bind us all together.

Mrs Thatcher, first of all, congratulations.
Thank you very much.

Ten years—it can't all have been easy.
It hasn't been easy by any means. We've had difficult moments, as is always the case in a long-running show.

What do you think have been the high points?
I don't know whether that's for me to say, but I greatly enjoyed the episodes we shot in Russia.

With Mikhail Gorbachev?
Yes. It was great working with him.

He is good, isn't he?
I think he's fantastic.

He looks good on screen.
Yes. I think the key thing is he doesn't do too much. He's very still.

He's very powerful, isn't he?
You feel it just walking around with him. What power! But it's restrained, you know—he's not out there using it all the time. There's such a sense of control.

Did you enjoy the Falklands episodes?
Loved them. I just loved them.

It rated well, didn't it?
Rated its britches off. It was bigger than Texas.

Who wrote those episodes?

The usual writers. Very good writers. We've always had very good writers.

Didn't you write some of that stuff yourself?

I wrote a bit. I was really just in at the storyboard stage.

Didn't you write the bit about the Belgrano?

How did you know about that? Yes, I did write that bit. That was supposed to be a secret. Someone's done their homework. Full marks!

That bit was hugely popular, wasn't it?

I've never seen anything like it. Everybody watched it. You'd go to work and no one talked about anything else.

Why did it work so well?

Oh, people love colour and movement. And remember, the country had been through some pretty bleak times. We needed something to bind us all together. It cheered us all up.

Did you go down there?

My stuff was mostly done in London.

Your part went extremely well, didn't it?

Yes, it did. We extended the show, went to another series on the strength of it…and here we are.

Weren't there some people hurt working on that whole Falklands thing?

Not in the London part of it, no.

No, down in the actual Falklands part of it?

Oh, down in the actual Falklands part of it? Yes, I think there were a couple of accidents down there. There were an awful lot of extras involved.

Weren't some ships sunk?

I think there was some small incidence of ships sinking, yes.

You didn't like playing opposite Arthur Scargill, did you?
It wasn't that I didn't like it—he simply wasn't any good. Couldn't remember his lines. Not very bright.

Cecil Parkinson's back in the series now, isn't he?
Yes, he is now. He was written out for a brief period.

Why?
Script problems, really. His secretary in the show, the little girl...I forget her name...

Sarah Keyes.
Sarah, that's right. She had a baby and, as it was written, he was the father. Well, Cecil didn't think he should have been the father. He was playing the sort of very faithful best-friend character and he didn't think his character would do that. He's back now, of course.

What's he playing?
He plays this sort of very faithful best-friend type who is more or less completely untrustworthy.

Did you think, when you started in the role, that you'd still be playing it ten years later?
Not for a minute. We thought it'd run for a couple of months, get the family in, a few friends, drink a bit of bubbly, and get off.

What do you think have been the ingredients?
Oh, a bit of pantomime, a bit of glamour, good writing, good guests—and some tough subjects. We did one on some unemployed kids not long ago.

How many kids?
About four and a half million of them, living up north somewhere.

This is a hard one, isn't it?
It's heartbreaking.

Is there an answer?
There has to be.

What is it?
Run the Falklands again. It worked the first time.

The Hon. Andrew Peacock
Re-Elected Leader of the Opposition

I am.

Mr Peacock, nice to have you back again. Who's the leader of the Liberal Party?

I am.

If the Liberal Party wins the next election, who's going to be the next prime minister?

I am.

If there is a television debate between you and Mr Hawke…are you with me?

I am.

…who is going to benefit from any mistake or miscalculation Mr Hawke might make, even though it might be very slight?

I am.

In fact, who's still talking about the last time it happened?

I am.

What's the name of the single beat in the conventional rhythm of English poetry?

Iamb.

Who's a pretty boy, then?

I am.

Are you aware of the revelations made on 'Four Corners' this week concerning the way your supporters got rid of Mr Howard?

I am.

When a group from the party comes to you like that, with a plot to knife a man you've sworn loyalty to, can I ask what your first priority is?
I am.

Are you in agreement that the next leader of your party will be Fred Chaney?
I am.

Are you aware that such a move is already on?
I am.

Mr Chaney's kept a very low profile during the week. A lot of people don't even know who he is. What's he got going for him, what's his biggest asset?
I am.

Mr Peacock, thanks for joining us again. Were those questions all right? They weren't too hard?
Pretty good. I thought you stuck to the point admirably.

Not too tough? I could do them again.
No, no.

Who's driving you home?
I am.

The Hon. Bob Hawke
Prime Minister of Australia

A totally unique experience.

Mr Hawke, it's been quite something this week, hasn't it?
It's been fantastic. It's been one of the great things you could ever go through as an Australian. I wouldn't have missed it for the world.

What do you think is the significance of the Gallipoli experience?
It's a unique experience in Australian history. A lot of lessons. I think the main lesson is that we as Australians have got to control our own destiny. We must never again allow ourselves to be put in the position of being ordered to do things by other people—not our idea, we don't control it, and frequently we're not even told the full story. It's a unique experience and that's a very valuable lesson.

Is the experience unique, though?
Totally unique in Australian history.

What about Bullecourt?
Aside from Bullecourt. Bullecourt was very like it.

Fromelles?
And Fromelles, yes. Aside from Bullecourt and Fromelles, totally unique.

And what about the Somme?
And the Somme. Take those three out and it's unique.

Passchendale?
Well, take the First War out, then. It's completely unique aside from the First War.

But what about Singapore?
And Singapore. First War—take them out and it's a totally unique experience.

Cassino?
And Cassino. Well, take the Second War out as well, take both wars out. Outside war, it is a totally unique experience.

What about Maralinga?
Outside war and Maralinga, obviously, but the lesson's the same at all times. We as Australians have got to control our own destiny. We must never again get in the position of being ordered to do things by a lot of other people.

On another subject, why is the consumption tax debate back on the agenda?
The OECD wants us to introduce one.

Why don't we export more wheat?
The Americans won't allow it.

Why don't we sell more beef?
The Japanese don't want us to.

What's happening at Narrungar?
I don't know, I haven't seen the forecast.

North West Cape?
Nobody knows what's happening there.

Finally, Mr Hawke, what about the boys who never came back, the diggers who never returned. What do you think they would think of Australia's position now?
I don't know, it's difficult to say. I'd be speculating.

Well, speculate. Would they be for it or against it?
Dead against it, I would think.

Yes. *(Looks out the porthole.)* **What's that big thing out there?**
That? That's a wing. There's another one out the other side.

Where?
(Both look.) Well, there was earlier.

Mr Nobby Clark
Managing Director of the
National Australia Bank

You're importing too much.

Nobby Clark, thanks for joining us.
Thank you. It's a pleasure to be here.

Nobby, you understand the economy.
We certainly do. We run it.

Will interest rates go up?
Difficult to say.

Will they go down?
No.

Well, will they stay the same?
No.

So they'll go up?
Very, very difficult to say.

In simple terms, what's wrong with the economy?
We have a slight problem in the current account at the moment.

What exactly is the current account?
The current account? Well, down one side you've got all the money Australia spends through importing, and on the other side you've got all the money Australia earns through exporting.

What's the position at the moment?
The position at the moment is that we're currently importing more than we export.

By how much?
By about 2000 million a month.

Whose fault is that?
It's your fault.

How can it be my fault? I don't import anything.
You're spending too much. The economy is overheated.

Well, how can I not spend? Everything costs a fortune.
You're importing too much. Are you buying Australian?

Yes, by and large.
Your clothes, for instance—are they Australian?

By and large, yes.
Do you drive a car?

No. I've got a Holden.
Have you got a CD player?

Yes, I have.
Have you got a television?

Yes, of course.
Have you got a computer?

Yes.
Are they Australian?

No.
Why not?

They don't make those things here.
Well, what have you got that's Australian?

I've got a blue pullover.
From Australian wool?

Yes.
A hundred per cent?

Yes.
An Australian 100 per cent fine wool jumper?

Yes.
Where did you get it?

Italy.
What else are you importing?

Nothing. More to the point, what are the banks importing?
We're not importing any goods at all.

Do you import profits?
No, we don't need to import profits.

Why not?
We're doing very nicely, thank you.

Well, do you import losses?
Import losses? How would we import a loss?

By running a bond market in Europe and running up debts so you owe money outside Australia.
Oh, I see—exporting part of our profit and diminishing our tax obligations.

Yes. Do you do that?
I've heard of that being done.

By you, Nobs?
I believe it was us I heard of doing it, yes, although I'm speaking from memory.

How much?
About one thousand million a month.

Who's going to pay for all this?
Ask me the first question again?

Nobs, are interest rates going up?
(Nobby winks.)

The Hon. Bob Hawke
Prime Minister of Australia

The system works fine.

Mr Hawke, this is a historic time, isn't it? The Berlin Wall is down, people are free to come and go across the borders for the first time in forty years.
Yes, it's a very exciting time.

The news looks like a mardi gras. Why are so many people leaving Australia?
They're only going for short periods, to have a look. Most of them will be back.

They don't look as though they're coming back. Isn't it time we admitted that capitalism doesn't work? It's out of date, isn't it?
The system works fine.

Don't people want freedom? Isn't that the point of what's happening? They don't want an authoritarian system.
They haven't got one.

Who runs the army?
The government.

Who runs the police?
The government.

Who runs the courts?
The judges.

Who runs the judges?
Nobody runs the judges—there's a fundamental concept of justice at work there.

Who got rid of Justice Staples?
The government, but we didn't get rid of the others.

Who runs the government?
It's a democracy. The people control the government. They vote.

When do they vote next?
I don't know.

Why not?
I haven't decided.

If they don't vote for your candidate, who do they vote for?
The other candidate.

From the other capitalist party?
Yes, there's a choice.

Why can't people afford houses?
Interest rates.

Who set that policy?
The government.

Who makes the money?
The banks.

Who runs the media?
Independent media groups in free competition with one another.

Who finances them?
The banks.

What's the problem with the national economy?
We owe too much money overseas.

What do you mean, 'we'? Who borrowed it?
Three or four bold entrepreneurs.

Why don't they pay it back?
They haven't got it any more. They're broke.

Who do they owe it to overseas?
The banks.

Will you be leaving, yourself?
Yes, next Tuesday.

Where are you going?
East Germany, Czechoslovakia, Hungary.

Who with?
The banks.

The Hon. Andrew Peacock
Leader of the Opposition

The reality is.

Mr Peacock, thanks for being here.
Thank you. It's a great pleasure. Thanks for coming.

I'm interviewing you.
Of course you are. Go ahead.

You've been talking about what the reality is.
Yes, the reality is. It's very important. The reality is. I've been saying that for six weeks.

What is it?
The reality.

Yes, but what is it?
What's the reality?

Yes.
It is.

I thought this was part of a longer statement: 'The reality is such and such.'
No. The reality isn't such and such. It is.

But Mr Hawke hasn't mentioned reality in the campaign.
Exactly.

Mr Peacock, he could hardly say that the reality isn't, could he?
I don't know what he's going to say. He hasn't said a word about it. He hasn't said it is. He hasn't responded to any of our other policies, either.

Such as?
We are.

We are what?
We are. Not 'We are what.' Watch my lips, son. 'We are.'

That's a policy?
You bet.

On what?
On a range of matters.

Mr Peacock, can I put this to you…
There's another one.

Sorry?
Defence policy.

That's a defence policy?
Of course it is. A very good one.

Do you have any other policies like that?
Plenty of them. Let me tell you this.

That's a policy?
Education policy.

With respect, Mr Peacock, these are all phrases. There's no content here.
Come on. You're playing semantics.

These are just useless phrases.
Obviously you've got to look at them in the context of the overall Liberal Party platform.

What is the Liberal Party platform?
The Liberal Party platform? Haven't you been listening for six weeks?

I have.
The Liberal Party platform.

But what is it?
The.

The?
The.

What's 'the'?
The?

What is it?
What do you mean, what's 'the'? It's the entire Liberal Party platform.
All these other things come from it.

Mr Peacock, thanks for joining us.
There's another one.

What?
Ethnic affairs policy.

Thanks for joining us.
It's a pleasure.

Is that a policy?
You bet.

What is that a policy on?
I'm not going to tell you. We're not announcing that until Tuesday.

Where?
There's another one.

Thanks a lot.
That's another one.

I'm going to have to go.
There's another one, although we're not bringing that in until the
second year.

The Hon. John Hewson
Leader of the Opposition

Trick me into a denial.

Dr Hewson, thank you for finding the studio.
Thank you. It's a great pleasure to arrive, and thank you for inviting
me.

You're working towards some proposal for a consumption tax.
What I actually said was, we are looking for a scenario where, under
certain circumstances, it may not be completely inappropriate to
introduce some sort of very broadly based consumption tax at some
future time.

How does a consumption tax work?
No, look…*(Conspiratorially.)* What you do is…I pretend that we're
not going to introduce a consumption tax and you try to trick me into
denying that we're going to do it. That's the way it works.

Dr Hewson, could you describe a consumption tax?
Why don't you do that? I say, 'We're not going to introduce one,' and
then…I'll help you, I'll give you a few clues. I'll leak some John Elliot
stuff. Then I'll say, 'Yes, of course, there is some support in some
quarters for some sort of tax at some future time.' That's the way the
consumption tax argument works. Read it out.

What is a consumption tax, Dr Hewson? Is it a tax on consumption?
Yes, of course it is.

**There are three things you can do with money, aren't there? You can
save it, spend it or invest it.**
That's right.

The poor don't save much.
They don't save a whole lot, no.

Do they make a lot of investments?
I don't think they're a very big player in the market currently. No.

So, a consumption tax is applied to money that is spent.
Correct.

Let me put this to you: if a family has an income, after paying income tax, of $500 a week, and it costs them $500 a week for rent, food and running the car; they have no investments, no savings; what percentage of their income attracts a consumption tax?
Roughly?

Roughly.
Roughly 100 per cent.

What are you going to do with all this money?
We're going to give tax relief.

To whom?
To people who save and invest...Why don't you trick me into a denial? That's the way the consumption argument works. Trick me into a denial that we're actually planning to introduce it. That's the way it works.

You want to play a game?
Yes. Why don't you play the game properly?

I don't want to play a game.
You big sook.

I beg your pardon?
You're a big baby.

The Hon. John Button
Minister for Industry, Technology and Commerce

I'm not going to say anything.

Senator Button, how do you think things are going?
Look, let me make it clear—I'm prepared to answer questions that relate directly to the portfolio of industry, but I'm not going to be drawn into any general speculative comment. I tried that last time and we haven't been able to use the fan for nearly a fortnight.

Is the Car Plan going to be affected by the Ford recall?
No. As I understand it they are only recalling a very small number of vehicles.

How small?
About 70,000.

A small number of 70,000?
Very small number of about 70,000 vehicles, for some very minor modifications, as I understand it.

What was the fault?
It wasn't a fault. 'Fault' is the wrong word—please stop using it. It is not a fault, it's a very minor modification in certain models.

What is it?
Something to do with the steering. It's a technical thing.

Where is the steering wheel?
It's in the boot, but only in certain models.

What about the imported ones?
The imported models are fine. Go ahead.

On another subject, were you consulted about the twenty per cent foreign ownership ceiling for TV?

No. I wasn't, but I've got great faith in the minister, Kerry Beazley. Kerry's done his homework very well and, frankly, I think he's made the right decision. We need to decide in this country whether we want our television to be dominated by foreigners.

What was the alternative?

Well, you can read a newspaper dominated by foreigners.

Radio?

Yes. Listen to that—dominated by foreigners.

Minister, can I ask you your opinion of the recent performance of the treasurer, Mr Keating?

No. You can't. I'm not going to speak about that at all. I've made that perfectly plain. How clear do you want it to be? I'm not going to say anything.

Senator Button, with respect, you must have a view.

I'm not going to tell you my view. I'm going to keep my view to…

Senator Button, you are the third highest minister in the country. You can't very well pretend not to have a view about the current macroeconomic climate.

I'm not going to say anything.

Can you give us some indication of it?

(Senator button holds up three fingers.)

Three words.

(Senator Button holds up two fingers.)

Second word…

(Senator Button flaps his elbows.)

Er…hen…

(Indicates rooster's comb.)

Male hen…rooster.
(Points up.)

Rooster…rooster up…up rooster…rooster-up.
(Holds up one finger.)

First word…
(Makes circle with hands.)

Whole…entire…complete.
(Indicates correct.)

Complete rooster-up.
Complete rooster-up! Good grief—I'll give you another go.
(Hands indicate movement of clock.)

Er…er…clock.
(Pulls ear.)

Sounds like clock. Cock! Complete rooster cock.
Complete rooster cock! *(Gives up in disgust, looks away.)* Next!

The Hon. Bob Hawke
Prime Minister of Australia

The doctors are absolutely delighted with my progress.

Prime Minister, you look great. How do you feel?
I'm a danger to shipping.

The doctors are pleased with your progress?
The doctors are absolutely delighted with my progress. All the indications are favourable. Yes.

With respect, that's the second time you've recovered this year, isn't it?
That's extremely amusing.

What actually happened, Mr Hawke?
You mean the operation?

Yes.
Oh, I don't want to talk about the operation. Let's talk about politics. You don't want to hear about an operation.

Why not?
Well, basically, it's plumbing. That's all it is. It's a very standard piece of carpentry and plumbing. Let's not bother with that. Let's talk about something else.

I just want to know precisely what happened during the operation.
I'd rather not talk about it. Can't we discuss something else?

Prime Minister, it's all very well going to press conferences and joking about small member's bills and the like. I think the public's got a right to know.
I did make some flippant remarks of a very childish nature prior to…I suppose I was a bit jumpy before the operation. I deeply regret those remarks now, of course.

Were you embarrassed?

I suppose I was a little bit embarrassed, yes. It's just not something I knew how to do and I suppose I had made a little bit of a fool of myself, but I don't want to go through analysis. If you really want to know what happened in the operation, I can tell you.

I'd like that. Go ahead, please.

In lay terms—without getting too technical about it—first of all, they knock you out, obviously. The next thing they do is make a very small incision somewhere in behind the Walshes; they pin the Tates back; they put the Dawkins out of the way, of course; they run any surplus Jones off into a bucket; and then they get a very small probe and they pull out, in my case, a little tiny Button about the size of the head of a pin.

What about the performance of Paul Keating?

Oh, they never get around that far. That doesn't come into it.

Why not?

Well, you're lying on your back. How would they do that?

Oh, I see.

I haven't explained myself very well. I mean, physiologically they couldn't possibly do that.

I see.

You're on your back. They can only get to the top part.

I see. Right.

Have you got a pencil?

Yes.

Here. I'll show you. *(Makes an illustration.)* First of all, there's your Dawkins. You've got the Walshes down here.

Yes.

They run a little probe up into here.

Yes.

They pin these Tate valves back.

Yes.

And they pull that out.

Yes.

Now, the Keating would be around here.

Oh, I see.

How would they get to that?

Mr David Hill
Professional Bureaucrat and Freelance Genius

Not as such, no.

Mr Hill, can I ask you, have you ever produced a television program?
Not personally, no.

Ever produced a film?
Not as such, no.

Have you ever written a film or a TV show?
No I haven't.

Did you ever design a set?
Not a set, no.

Any costumes?
Not costumes specifically.

Are you a member of Actors' Equity?
Not at the moment.

What about directing? Have you ever directed a film?
Not yet, no.

How about editing?
I've never done any editing at all.

Mixing?
What exactly is mixing?

Did you ever work in make-up?
No.

Were you ever a grip?
A grip? No.

Gaffer?
No. I don't, thanks.

Ever worked with computer graphics?
Ironically, no.

Overseas sales?
Never heard of them.

Have you ever production-managed?
Are you looking for a yes–no answer?

Yes.
No.

Have you ever been a lighting director or cameraman?
Which one?

Either.
No.

What about sound-recording?
What about it?

Have you ever done it?
Professionally?

Yes.
No.

Non-professionally?
Sound-recording?

Yes.
No.

Have you ever worked as a film or television critic?
Not in the sense of actually doing it, no.

What is your current occupation?
I am the chief executive of the Australian Broadcasting Corporation.

The Hon. Paul Keating
Celebrated Backbencher, Previously World's Greatest Treasurer

And to say nothing of the fact.

Mr Keating, thanks for coming in.
Well, thank you for inviting me in.

Lovely to see you again.
It's great to be back. Thank you very much.

I wondered if I could ask about the figures that were released this week.
The inflation figures? The June quarter inflation figures?

Yes, and the unemployment figures.
The ten per cent?

Yes.
Coupled with the twenty-eight per cent figure for teenage unemployment?

Yes.
Not to mention the hundreds of thousands of people who don't even bother to register.

Yes.
And neither to mention the financial burden of having 700,000 people on the dole.

Yes.
And to say nothing of the fact that men are falling out of the workforce at a rate higher than that of women.

Yes.

Because you don't have to pay women so much. So you get a deregulated labour market.

Yes.

And you've got a hundred thousand new migrants coming in every year.

Yes.

Just to swell the figure.

Yes.

Well, what about interest rates? Would you like to talk about that?

Yes.

Which they're refusing to lower?

Yes.

In case they imperil the economic miracle?

Yes.

And what about the American wheat sales? You want to talk about that?

Yes.

Which are robbing us of our two major markets?

Yes.

Which they said they'd never do because they're totally opposed to any form of regulation or centralised planning in an economy?

Yes.

In fact, they're pretending to be totally in favour of free trade and open competition?

Yes.

And while they're also pretending to be our friends?

Yes.

In fact, whenever they want anything, Bob's got to bend over, quick as look at you, for his pal George?

Yes.

'Here are three ships, George, and I think it's your putt?'

Yes, yes.

And why we've got no opposition in Canberra at all?

Yes.

First sign of anything wrong in the current account and you've Peter Reith coming out on to the parliament steps and giving us another demonstration of his accent?

Yes.

'I've been to all the right schools, I just can't remember why.'

Yes.

No, I don't want to talk about any of that.

Why not?

I caused it.

The Hon. Bob Hawke
Prime Minister of Australia

I don't need a lecture about Christian ethics.

Mr Hawke, thanks for joining us.
Thank you for inviting me.

You gave Archbishop Hollingworth a caning this week.
Oh, I don't know that I gave him a caning.

Mr Hawke, you gave him a caning.
Look, the man has to understand to stay out of the economic debate.
He's an archbishop; it's all very well for him to favour us with a few
noble observations, but he should stay out of the debate. I'm not
running an ideal world, I'm running a real economy, in a real country,
in the real world.

**But surely, Mr Hawke, he has the right to criticise an apparent
shortcoming in government policy?**
I didn't say he doesn't have the right to do that. I said he doesn't know
what he's talking about. He knows absolutely nothing about economics.

**Do you have to be an economist to have an opinion about the way the
country's being run?**
Well, obviously you've got to know something about economics if you're
going to make statements that bear on the economic debate. If you
don't, your comments are going to be irrelevant. Now the archbishop's
were, and I took the liberty of pointing that out to him.

**But if your economics program can't accommodate a basic level of
caring for the people that live here, surely the policy must be changed.
That's what he was arguing.**
Does anybody disagree with that? That's just a rhetorical statement.
Do we need an archbishop to point that out to us? Frankly, I don't
need a lecture about Christian ethics. I grew up with the Christian
morality; I don't need it described to me. Who was it for instance, in

this country, who got up and promised to get rid of child poverty? Who was that?

Mr Hawke, it hasn't happened.
It hasn't happened yet.

You said it was going to happen by the beginning of this year.
It hasn't happened by the beginning of this year yet.

But Mr Hawke...
Who was it—let me finish—who was it who got up in this country and quite openly wept, quite openly wept for the massacre of the innocents in Tiananmen Square? Was that the archbishop?

That was you.
That was me. Who was it who *again* quite openly got up, and confessed *freely* to having fooled around with other women and hopped into the turps slightly as a younger man? Was that the archbishop?

The archbishop probably wasn't unfaithful to his wife.
Well, is that my fault? Am I to be crucified because some archbishop didn't monkey about with other women?

Mr Hawke, I'm sorry I doubted you.
Are you happy?

(Sotto voce.) Yeah.
If it's all right with you, I think I'll go.

OK.
Open the door. *(Door opens to thunderous Hallelujah chorus.)* Have you got any bread and perhaps a bit of fish?

Surely to God you're not going to try and feed all of them out here?
No, of course not.

What are you going to do?
I'm going to make myself a sandwich; I haven't had any lunch.

A BHP Spokesman

I'll tell you something about your whale.

Thanks for joining us.
Thank you very much for inviting me in, Jana, it's a very great pleasure to be here.

No, I'm sorry, I'm not Jana.
Oh I'm sorry, I'm in the wrong place. *(Gets up to leave.)*

No, no, this is *A Current Affair*. I'm not Jana.
Oh I see. Well, thank you very much for inviting me in, Not Jana, it's a great pleasure.

Fine. You're having a dispute with Greenpeace over your exploration off the coast.
Well, yes, there is some ground between us left to cover. The precise detail you see of what we're doing seismically is somewhat at odds with the general principles espoused by Greenpeace, general principles, I might say, which we also espouse, general principles the espousal of which would be axiomatic, I would think, to any understanding of environmental issues.

Yes. Could you be more specific?
Yes, we were going to dig a dirty great hole in the seabed because there's a quid in it, and we got caught and we're rather embarrassed about it.

What does Greenpeace say is wrong with what you're doing?
They say the area we want to dig up is a whale-breeding area.

Is it?
No, it's not.

It isn't?
No. Well, that is to say, it won't be.

When won't it be?
It won't be when the whales get out of the area, will it?

Where are the whales going to go?
I don't know. I don't even know if there are any whales there.

Isn't it a breeding ground, though?
I've never seen any whales breeding out there.

Well, have you been out there?
Of course I've been out there. I was there the other day.

On a whale-spotting boat?
No, on a dirty great big new drilling rig we've got that can displace an area the size of India in an hour and a half. Fantastic thing.

And there were no whales breeding?
I didn't see any.

Did you hear any?
I beg your pardon?

Where are they going to breed then?
I don't know, but I can tell you something, they don't breed in the sea out there.

Where other than the sea out there do you think whales breed?
I don't know about whale-breeding. I'm not making myself clear: dirty great big holes in the seabed I can do for you; knowledge about whales I don't have. I'll tell you something about your whale: he's not a moron. The whale is a highly intelligent critter; I've seen them go through hoops at Sea World. Your whale's got enough brain to get out of the area while we're drilling, for goodness sake.

Can I put it another way? Is there oil out there under the seabed?
We don't know but we currently think so.

Have you got shares in BHP? Are you a shareholder?
Yes, of course I am.

Have you got shares in whales?
No, you can't get shares in whales, son. You don't buy shares in whales. Horses, yes, whales, no. I've got a share in a horse.

And how do you get a return from that?
They breed. You breed them. Why would you breed a whale? Your whale's got no speed and he can't stay; he's no good over hurdles your whale, and he's useless on the flat.

Thanks for joining us.
Have you ever backed a whale? I can't remember when I've ever backed a whale.

We're out of time, I'm sorry.
You'll get decent odds, son, but keep your money in your pocket.

Senator Bob Collins
Minister for Shipping

The front fell off.

Senator Collins, thanks for coming in.
It's a great pleasure, thank you.

This ship that was involved in the incident off Western Australia this week...
The one the front fell off? That's not very typical, I'd like to make that point.

How was it untypical?
Well, there are a lot of these ships going round the world all the time, and very seldom does this happen. I just don't want people thinking tankers aren't safe.

Is this tanker safe?
Well, I was thinking more about the other ones.

The ones that are safe?
Yes. The ones the front doesn't fall off.

If this tanker isn't safe, why did it have 80,000 tonnes of oil in it?
I'm not saying it wasn't safe, it's just perhaps not quite as safe as some of the other ones.

Why?
Well, some of them are built so the front doesn't fall off at all.

Wasn't this one built so that the front doesn't fall off?
Obviously not.

How do you know?
Because the front fell off, and 20,000 tonnes of crude oil spilt and the sea caught fire. It's a bit of a giveaway. I'd just like to make the point that that is *not* normal.

What sort of standards are these sea tankers built to?
Oh, very rigorous maritime engineering standards.

What sort of thing?
Well, the front's not supposed to fall off for a start.

And what other things?
There are regulations governing the material they can be made of.

What materials?
Well, cardboard's out.

And?
No cardboard derivatives.

Paper?
No paper. No string, no Sellotape.

Rubber?
No, rubber's out. They've got to have a steering wheel. There's a minimum crew requirement.

What's the minimum crew?
Oh—one I suppose.

So the allegation that they're just designed to carry as much oil as possible and to hell with the consequences, that's ludicrous, is it?
Absolutely ludicrous. These are very, very strong vessels.

So what happened in this case?
Well, the front fell off in this case, by all means, but it's very unusual.

But Senator Collins, why did the front fall off?
A wave hit it.

A wave hit it?
A wave hit the ship.

Is that unusual?
Oh yes. At sea? Chance in million!

So what do you do to protect the environment in cases like this?
Well, the ship was towed outside the environment.

Into another environment.
No, no, it's been towed beyond the environment. It's not in the environment.

What's out there?
Nothing's out there.

There must be something out there.
Look, there's nothing out there—all there is is sea, and birds, and fish.

And?
And 20,000 tonnes of crude oil.

And what else?
And a fire.

Anything else?
And the part of the ship that the front fell off. But there's nothing else out there.

Senator Collins, thank for joining us.
It's a complete void.

Yes. We're out of time.
The environment's perfectly safe. We're out of time? Can you book me a cab?

But didn't you come in a Commonwealth car?
Well, yes, I did.

What happened?
The front fell off.

Sir Joh Bjelke-Petersen
Premier of Queensland (1725–1987)

There was always a lot of laughter in our home.

Sir Joh, when was it you first realised that you could make other people laugh? Was it the schoolyard thing?
Yes, I suppose it was. It's a defensive thing. There's always the bully, isn't there? You've got to do something about it and with me it was always just making the other kids laugh.

You had trouble with authority at school I think, didn't you?
Not initially, but I changed schools when I was about eleven and I lost all my old friends and had to make new ones, and there was a teacher who made every attempt to goad me into insurrection so I could be punished within the law. In fact, if I'm on about anything, it's injustice.

Do you remember anything in particular that you did in those days?
A fellow who is now a meat-wholesaler and I once put a big sack of flour in the school chapel's air-conditioning during the annual re-enactment of the Easter Passion. That was good.

If we can talk now about some of those very 'Joh' things, the mannerisms, the little bits of verbal business that everyone hears and just thinks straight away 'That's Joh'.
You're thinking particularly of the 'Goodness me's and the 'Don't you worry about that's and so on?

Exactly.
The apparent confusion?

Yes.
Some of that was there very early.

How early?
I think we're probably talking fresh out of school here. I noticed that a lot of people, just in their normal speech, are inclined to fumble about a

bit and that, by exaggerating, I was able to strike a chord. I didn't very often use a script in those days either, which is another thing. And it's quite handy to have all your ideas just pile up and crash into each other because it gives you time to think, as well as, hopefully, with any real luck, getting a decent-sized laugh.

I know you've probably been asked this a thousand times before, but who are the other comics you most admire?
Oh, Joan Rivers.

She's great.
I mean, can we talk? The woman's fantastic. The first time I saw her: heart attack.

Yes.
Really. Literally. Off the bed on to the floor, rolling about, in a ball, need for air, the full catastrophe.

But not an influence as such.
No, I don't think so. Different style, different subject matter.

Who did influence you then?
Well, I think my parents. There was always a lot of laughter in our home and I think that's terribly important. The Keystone Cops.

The chaos?
Yes, the way a chase would just start up and people would be chasing, no reason, no nothing and there'd be haystacks with people's running legs sticking out of them. And I suppose to a great extent I've tried to do that with language.

It is often said that there is a fine line between comedy and tragedy. Do you believe that?
My word.

Are you the sad clown? The *commedia dell'arte* clown?
Well, I think I'm a very Australian clown. I think I'm a *very* Australian clown. I'm not immune to life's bleaker side, obviously, but I don't think

I'm consumed by it, either. I frequently find, for instance, the things which worry people, a lot, a lot of the things which worry people very badly, I find very funny. Personally, I find them very, *very* funny, and I wouldn't want that to sound as if I don't care.

I didn't take it in that sense.
Good.

Before we go, Sir Joh, you've made a lot of great humour in your time. You have a lot of great jokes. Which joke would you consider to be the joke, of all the ones you've performed?
That's a difficult question, just casting my mind back now, as we speak. There is great emotional pull for me, for the car that ran on water. I always thought that was very funny.

Yes.
Very, very funny. But I suppose in terms purely of audience response, sheer laughter, which is the ultimate measure of this thing, when I ran for prime minister.

Yes, that was always my favourite.
Thanks. I thought that went pretty well. I thought it was pretty funny.

Why do you think it actually worked as well as it did?
Various factors. First of all, let me say that it had been done before. It wasn't an original idea, people had been…

But you brought something to it, didn't you?
Well, I like to think so. I had a lot of luck with the timing. For instance, for a start I announced I was running for prime minister when there wasn't an election on.

Yes.
Pretty funny. Pretty funny.

Yes, it was.
Right from the kick-off, I mean that is pretty funny. Then, an election was called, and where was I?

Disneyland.
Disneyland. Pretty funny. Pretty funny. Pretty funny. You've got to say that's pretty funny. I had a lot of luck with the timing. It couldn't have been better for me. There I am running for prime minister when there's *no* election and then there *is* an election and I'm at Disneyland, being photographed with big-nosed people in the background and speaking of my personal…I mean it was pretty funny.

Couldn't believe your luck.
Couldn't believe my luck. On a plate. Literally on a plate.

Sir Joh, thank you very much for your time.
Thank you, you've been a wonderful audience.

Senator Gareth Evans
Minister for Foreign Affairs

We did nothing at all.

Senator Evans, thanks for coming in.
Thank you very much, it's a great pleasure to be here.

I'd like to talk about the events that took place this week in East Timor.
Well, yes, technically speaking of course it's not East Timor. It's part of Indonesia.

Well, a number of Timorese people were killed this week by the Indonesian Army. What is Australia's attitude to this question?
Well, let me go back a bit. When Indonesia liberated the freedom-loving people of East Timor in 1975, Australia of course was led by Gough Whitlam.

Who was later sacked.
Who was later sacked, indeed, although not quite as badly as East Timor was.

And what did Australia do?
We watched developments very closely and immediately did nothing.

We did nothing at all?
We did nothing at all. We did it immediately and we remained dedicated to an eloquence which I think can only flow from lengthy periods of complete silence.

How did this affect the military takeover?
Of a very small and relatively powerless East Timor by the biggest standing army in Asia?

Yes.
It went ahead as if absolutely nothing had happened.

A fair reading of the position.
As it happened, yes, an uncanny reading of our attitude at that time.

What have we done since?
Since then we've remained completely consistent with the determinations made steadfastly and with the highest possible motivation at that time.

We've continued not to do anything?
I wouldn't have put it like that.

How would you put it?
I wouldn't put it at all. I'm a member of the Australian government. Our policy is not to put anything at all at any time.

If you had to put it, how would you put it?
Well, I would say we've remained completely consistent with the central tenets of an arrangement going back over a period of time and we've made a measured and very carefully worded response.

We've done nothing?
It's a lot more carefully worded than that.

How carefully worded?
Look, there are 180 million Indonesians—how carefully worded do you want it to be?

So we don't do anything?
We are with the central Asian island republics in the sense of a commonality of purpose *(Interviewer packs up and leaves.)* in the theatre of central Asian economic and political development. And if we're going to talk about the current position up there, by which I… *(Interviewer leaves studio.)*…there is a position which one could quite sensibly submit which suggests that these ideas are felt more keenly perhaps in Jakarta even than they are here, in Fantasyland. *(Looks around.)* Where on earth has everybody gone?

A Primate of the Church

As we move forward into the twelfth century.

Thanks for joining us.
It's a pleasure.

I wonder if I could ask you, as the primate of the church, about your opposition to the ordination of women...
Could I just pause there momentarily? You say, 'as the primate of the church'...was that the expression you used?

I thought you were the primate of the church.
No, I'm *a* primate in the church but I'm certainly not *the* primate.

How many primates are there?
In the church?

Yes.
There are many thousands of them obviously. Some of them are opposed to the ordination of women and then there's a completely different group, of course, who are dead against it.

Are you opposed to the ordination of women?
Yes, I am, and could I preempt your next question by saying that this is not a discriminatory thing against, ahm...

Women.
Pardon?

Women.
Where?

No, the discrimination, it's not against women.
Oh no, there's nothing they can do about it. How can they help it? It's just bad luck.

Why are the primates you hang around with opposed to the ordination of women? Aren't some of the primates in favour of the ordination of women?

Yes, some of them are, but more of the ones I hang about with are opposed to it.

Why?

Because it's unconstitutional. The constitution of the church specifically forbids it.

But surely the constitution can be changed?

Under certain circumstances that's possible.

How?

Well, the expression for instance, 'as we move forward into the twelfth century', that was changed.

To 'the twentieth'.

Well, that's a fairly radical suggestion, but we'd certainly give you a hearing.

The point I'm trying to make here is, aren't you cutting the church off from society at the very time when it needs to become relevant to the community?

I beg your pardon. The church is going through a very successful phase at the moment.

Aren't numbers down?

Numbers are not down, no. I was at the church this afternoon and the turnout was extremely encouraging.

What was the occasion?

The occasion will interest you, actually. It was the birthday of one of our very youngest members in the congregation: young Terry.

How old was he?

Young Terry?

Yes.
He'd be eighty-seven.

Look, can I ask where you're going to get people entering the ministry if you're not going to allow women who are otherwise fully qualified to get in?
Obviously we're going to recruit from the ranks of men.

But where are they going to come from?
There are plenty of people. I, for instance, could have a try.

You could be ordained as a minister?
Of course.

But what are your qualifications?
(Rising from seat, his hand goes towards his fly.) I'll show you my qualifications. *(Freeze.)*

A Newspaper Editor From Sydney

We think it's time Australia grew up.

Thanks for coming in.
It's a pleasure to be here, thank you.

Can I ask you, as editor of one of the major daily newspapers, do you support the idea of Australia becoming a republic?
Yes, we do, but I should point out that we're not the only player in the market obviously, and I can only speak for our organisation. We don't have the whole market.

How much of it do you have?
At the moment?

Yes.
Ninety-three per cent at the moment, but we're talking to the government. We think it's a bit restrictive.

So as a newspaper do you support the republican push?
Yes, we do, by and large. We think it's time Australia grew up. We're not English. We're Australian. Different hemisphere, different country, different history, completely different pattern of post-war migration. We think it's time we matured, and walked into the sunlit upland of our own destiny. Incidentally, did you know that Fergie and Randy Andy have given it away?

Do you think the republican issue will figure in the federal election?
Yes, we do, we think it's probably one of the main issues that's going to dominate in the next couple of months, here's a photo of Fergie with a bloke from America. *(Holds photo to interviewer.)* The old Andy was away on manoeuvres if you know what I mean, nudge kick wink, say no more. Here's another one. This is a beauty—you tell me what that is. *(Hands him another photo.)* That is Princess Di's knee. That's taken from the back. Nude.

Princess Di's knee?
Now, can you tell me where Charlie Boy is in that photo? Can you see a bloke who looks like the FA Cup? He's not there, is he?

He's not there. What does this mean?
Could be all over for another royal marriage, couldn't it? Of course, the person I bleed for is the queen.

So you're swinging right behind the movement to make Australia a republic?
Absolutely. We're rock solid behind the republican movement, don't worry about that.

Is it in tomorrow's paper?
High, wide and handsome in tomorrow's paper, yes.

Have you got a headline?
Huge headline; huge headline.

What is it?
GET OFF OUR BACKS, POMMY MONGRELS. QUEEN'S DOG FARTS AT RACES.

Anything about racism?
Racism is all finished, isn't it? Went out of existence.

Not there anymore?
Didn't they vote it out of existence on Wednesday night?

In South Africa, yes, but what about here?
Well, it wouldn't happen here. I'd have noticed it in the paper. I run it.

Yeah, sure. Thanks for joining us.
Have you heard about Prince Edward?

No.
You know he's a teapot?

A what?
I'm a republican myself, of course.

The Keating Miracle

20 December 1991 – 11 March 1996

Mr Keating, thanks for coming in.
Thanks very much for inviting me in, it's a great
pleasure and an honour and a privilege, anything
I can do to help...

You've been in the new job for some time now...
...if I can say that without being patronising, or
appearing arrogant.

Without what?
I'm just slightly alarmed by the idea that people
think of me as a little bit on the arrogant side.

This is what the polls are saying?
Yes, although you've got to have a look at who they're
asking.

The Australian public.
Well, exactly.

Mr Alan Bond
Retired Yachtsman

A very exciting new development in Western Australia.

Mr Bond, thanks for coming in.
I'm not in yet. The matter is still proceeding. I'm still out at the moment.

But you're appealing.
That's very kind. Thanks very much.

I mean your lawyers are appealing.
A lot of people don't think so but I think they're pretty good. I think they're doing a very good job.

You didn't have much of a week, did you?
Couldn't take a trick earlier, but things perked up a bit today.

You're not on the list of Australia's ten richest people anymore.
No, I'm not, but you'll note that two of my sons are.

Really? What do they do?
Do? They don't do anything, they're among the richest people in the country.

But where did they get the money?
Well, it's old money.

What old money?
Any old money, frankly, that we could still find lying about.

So what are you doing now?
I've got plenty on. I've got a very exciting new development in Western Australia. Lovely new units that were just finalised today. I can fit you in there, if you're interested in investing in units.

What is it?
It's in South Perth, beautifully positioned, all self-contained, exquisite, government-backed.

How many bedrooms?
One bedroom, but it's got the lot, everything's in there and there's a sort of a communal area where all of the facilities are housed. It's a totally new concept in urban dwelling.

So it's like a retirement village type of idea?
It's very like a retirement village type of idea, yes, for business people in Australia who are a bit jaded after a lifetime of service to the community.

Like yourself.
Yes.

And is it quiet?
Oh, very quiet, yes. Someone could scream to death in the next room and you wouldn't hear a sausage.

What about a view?
Yes, beautiful views. Panoramic views.

So the units are elevated?
No, the windows are elevated.

Security?
Oh, groaning with security. You can't get in, the walls are this thick and there's a guard on the gate. Very secure.

And are they expensive?
I could do you one for about 280, 275, best price 260.

Mmm. Is there any interest from overseas or is it a local project?
Yes, there is interest overseas, we've got somebody from Spain coming into one of the units, probably later this year. Into the Penthouse unit.

Oh, so there's an upper level.
No actually, there isn't, but he didn't know that when he bought it.

But you expect them to sell pretty well.
I expect them to be chocka by Christmas at the present rate.

And so anyone interested should get in touch with you?
Yes. Contact my office. Speak to Mr G. Overnor, he's managing the property for us.

Mr Overnor.
Yes, or Mr D. Eputygovernor if he's busy.

Is there a deposit?
There is in some of the units, yes, but we'll clean them out pretty severely before you come in.

And so you're still very busy.
I've got plenty of ideas, I've got a swag of stuff to get through.

Like what?
I've got to redirect the mail, get a toothbrush, talk to the milkman—I've got a list here somewhere—cancel the papers. I've got plenty of things to do.

Well, Alan Bond, see you again.
Eh?

See you again.
How soon do you reckon?

The Hon. Barry Jones
Chairman of the Australian
Labor Party
Parent–Teacher Night

A great deal more homework.

Mr Jones, thanks for coming in.
Thank you very much, and good evening.

And congratulations on your appointment this week.
Thank you very much, difficult job, great challenge.

You're lucky to have a job.
That's true, good thing I'm not young, I wouldn't have stood a chance.

It's not going to be easy taking over in the middle of the year, is it?
No, it isn't, and of course they've got some very serious tests coming up; we'll need to get on with it.

So you'll be keeping the work up to them, will you?
I will, and I think they need a much more structured program.

Will this involve more homework?
Probably a great deal more homework, yes; was there anyone in particular you were interested in?

Paul. Paul Keating.
Paul Keating. Well, Paul as you know is a bright enough lad and greatly enjoying being head boy, after being deputy head for so long.

But is he getting any work done? We don't see any evidence of anything significant that he's doing.
Well, he's certainly been putting in the hours. Did you see the project he did on cable television, for instance?

Yes, we did.
Did a great deal of work but he didn't answer the question. I mean, he needs to organise himself. Did you have a chance to talk to him about that project?

We tried, but he kept changing his mind all the time about what he thought.
I don't think he thought *anything*, did he? There was no evidence of it.

He seems to be a member of some sort of gang.
Well, boys of that age, you know what they're like; some of these boys are perfectly all right, some of them are a bit of a problem.

What about this young Richardson?
Graham Richardson? A typical example, and he may have to repeat a year I think.

John Dawkins?
Paul and John have been helping each other with their maths, haven't they?

Yes, but they both got an F.
That's true. They didn't exactly bolt in, did they?

Well, is there anything we can do at home?
Does Paul read a lot? He doesn't strike me as being a well-informed boy.

We hardly ever see him. He's never home.
Perhaps you should take him out, introduce him to some kids, some unemployed kids. I'm sure they'd love to talk to somebody like Paul.

I don't think so; he hides in his bedroom and he won't come out.
Look, we'll do what we can; obviously we'll be giving him extra maths, extra English.

Extra history.
Extra history, by all means.

Economics?

I don't think Paul's doing economics is he? No, he's not down here as having anything to do with economics.

Yes, yes he is. He told us he was doing economics today.

No. Double sport, lunch, and a school visit to a piggery this afternoon.

But he told us he was coming top in it.

As far as I know he's not doing economics at all.

We thought he was coming in dux.

Oh, we don't pry into their private lives. I mean the school can't do everything.

The Hon. John Hewson
Leader of the Opposition

My personal popularity is breathtaking.

Dr Hewson, thank you for coming in.
Thank you for inviting me.

Support for the coalition parties is sixteen percentage points above that for the government.
Yes, support for the conservative parties at the moment is very high indeed.

And your popularity is up, as well.
My personal popularity is breathtaking.

You must be very pleased with this.
I'm a very pleased person. I'm delirious with happiness.

And why do you think this is?
Well, because we've got a good team, and good solid, strong, derisive leadership.

Decisive.
I beg your pardon?

Decisive.
Who is?

You are.
Who says?

The polls.
Are you serious? What, I'm considered a good leader in Poland?

No, no, here, in the popularity polls.
Oh, in Australia? I'm sorry.

What are you going to do? Are you going to make some announcements, stir things up a bit?
Oh no, I'm not going to *say* anything. I wouldn't say anything.

Why on earth not?
My popularity will go down if I say anything. That's been the pattern. I've only got one advantage: I'm not Bob Hawke. That's why I'm popular. If I say anything, my popularity goes down. I announced that we were sending the troops into the wharves and my popularity went down. I can't afford to say anything.

If we could talk about that: you were going to send in the army?
Well, aerial bombardment first, obviously, but then send in the army, yes.

You were going to run bombing raids?
High-level bombing raids, yes, just to soften them up before we send the troops in before the ground war starts. You've got to soften the enemy up.

And what about nuclear weapons?
Well, I wouldn't rule them out. This is a very serious position.

You would seriously think about nuking the waterfronts?
Well, I think we might have to; this is a very serious business. Do you realise that in Singapore they can turn a ship around in five hours? Five hours to turn a ship completely around!

And how long do we take?
In Australia?

Yes.
It'll be four years on Saturday.

Do you think there'll be any collateral damage here?
Well, we may lose a Peter Reith or two, but I don't think anything serious will happen.

Why Peter Reith?
Well, because we say he's an essential aspect of the future plan of course.

And what do they say?
They think he's a milk treatment plant.

And what is he in actuality?
In actuality he's a decoy, we get them made up in Switzerland. They're very good. They look like Peter Reith, they sound like Peter Reith, they've got the same thickness as Peter Reith, which is...

...fairly thick.
Fairly extreme. But they're not a fully operational Peter Reith. Have you ever seen Peter Reith?

Yes, of course.
Fully inflated?

I don't think I've seen him any other way.
Well, we've got cupboards full of them.

Is that right?
Yeah. If something goes wrong we get another one of them. You can see the join if you know what you're looking for.

And what are you looking for?
Somebody to replace Peter Reith.

The Hon. John Dawkins
Treasurer of Australia

I don't keep saying the same thing.

Mr Dawkins, thanks for joining us.
Thank you, it's a pleasure to be here.

I wonder if I could ask you about the economic recovery.
By all means, what would you like to know about it?

In what century do you think it'll happen?
Well, I think we're already beginning to get certain initial indications that the start of what we hope might be an economic recovery...

Mr Dawkins...
...is beginning to manifest itself in certain pockets of the economic model...

Mr Dawkins...
...I think the situation's really quite hopeful.

Mr Dawkins, how do you think the recovery will be affected by the next ice age?
The problem you see is that we're in the grip of a global recession and I think people appreciate that...

Mr Dawkins...hullo, hullo?
...and I think that the microeconomic reform program we've embarked on is going to strengthen the fundamental model...

Mr Dawkins? It doesn't matter what I ask you, does it?
So that when the economic recovery does begin to bite we'll be in a much stronger overall position.

Mr Dawkins, did you get to the football the other night?
We've got short-term interest rates pegged to around 6.5 per cent,
which of course means...

Mr Dawkins, wave if you can hear me.
...which of course means that when recovery does begin to bite it will
be sustainable in terms of low inflation.

Mr Dawkins, you keep saying the same thing all the time.
I don't keep saying the same thing.

You keep saying the same thing.
I don't keep saying the same thing.

You keep saying the same thing.
I *don't* keep saying the same thing.

Mr Dawkins...
I do not keep saying the same thing.

...you keep saying the same thing.
I don't keep saying the same thing, certainly not all the time.

**Mr Dawkins, what about the people? What are you supposed to do in
this country if you're not a major financial institution?**
Well, look, I'm running Treasury; we operate on a pretty big scale up
there, I don't quite know what you're talking about.

**You keep saying the same thing. I'm talking about things like youth
unemployed.**
There are no youth unemployed.

Mr Dawkins...
There are, by all means, rather a lot of non-elderly transitional units
in the Australian employment market but youth unemployment in
Australia is among the lowest in the OECD.

How low?
Four.

Four per cent?
No, four people.

Four young people out of work?
Four or five. It may have crept as high as five.

What about education, social welfare, small business, health?
Well, hang on, you've mentioned three or four other portfolios there.
Why don't you speak to these other ministers?

Mr Dawkins, you know that it's all indexed to the economy. What are you going to do?
Why don't you get a grant and turn this into a movie?

How would I do that?
Apply. Do you know anyone in Treasury?

No.
Oh well, you haven't got a chance. There's your problem.

Mr Dawkins, thanks for joining us.
Mmm?

Mr Dawkins, thanks for joining us.
Don't you know *anyone* in Treasury?

Well, I know you.
Yes, but I just keep saying the same thing.

The Australian Olympic Coach
Live from Barcelona

They've been training day and night.

Thanks for joining us.
(Live, via satellite, from Barcelona.) Thank you very much, it's a pleasure.

How's the weather?
Lovely day today. Beautiful day.

And how do you think we'll do?
Well, the swimming people are very pumped up. You'd probably recognise all the usual names. We've got John Dawkins in the backstroke. I think that's Tuesday night.

He's from the Institute, isn't he?
Oh very much so, yes. And with a very unusual style.

What's that?
Well, he swims in the backstroke, but he actually swims feet first; he gets in the water backwards and he kicks off with his head.

And wasn't he having trouble with his turns?
Yes, he doesn't actually do turns, he just swims up to the end, bumps his head and stops.

What for?
He says he's waiting for someone to turn the pool around.

And what's his best time?
Early afternoon he's probably not bad.

Have you seen anything of John Hewson?
John Hewson and the synchronised swimming team?

Yes.
Yes, they've been training day and night. They're at a bit of a disadvantage unfortunately, over here.

Oh, why's that?
Well, they've noticed that when they dive in, some of the other teams competing over here come up again.

So they've got a bit of work to do?
Unless they can get synchronised drowning recognised as a sport by Thursday it's probably curtains, yes.

And how's Paul Keating doing?
I saw Paul today. He's looking pretty fit, very good. He's in the decathlon, of course, and quietly confident in all three events.

But the decathlon has ten events.
That's what it says in the program but Paul doesn't agree with the figures.

Is Gareth Evans looking good?
Gareth Evans isn't actually convinced that the Olympics are on. He thinks it's a press beat-up.

So what's he saying?
Well, he's saying that this is the sort of thing that happens from time to time and there's …

…nothing anybody can do about it…
…nothing anybody can do about it, and he's had an incredible response from the Indonesians…

…from the Indonesians, yes. And just finally, how's Bill Kelty doing?
Bill's not here yet; unfortunately he seems to have got the venue off a chart in the ACTU office and he hasn't turned up yet. We heard from him today.

Where from?
He's in Helsinki.

Right. So it's gold, gold, gold, eh?
I beg your pardon?

Gold, gold, gold.
No, it's pretty warm here. Lovely day today.

The Hon. Paul Keating
Prime Minister of Australia

This is a recession-driven recovery.

Mr Keating, thanks for coming in.
Pleasure.

Could you explain the significance of the figures released this week?
Yes, the indications are that we're in recovery, which is completely consistent with government projections, and very gratifying after what I think has been a difficult time for everyone.

It's not a very strong recovery, though, is it?
It's a good recovery, yes. It's driven by private demand, which is what we wanted.

Why did demand increase?
People are having sales. Businesses have dropped their prices to get rid of stock. They've had to. There's a recession on out there, don't you read the papers?

Has inflation gone up?
No, that's what's so fantastic. That's why the recovery has come about.

Why hasn't inflation gone up if demand has gone up?
Because prices haven't gone up. Prices have dropped. That's the only reason there's any demand at all.

And that tends to keep inflation down?
Oh yes.

And this is because of the recession?
Oh yes.

So the cause of the recovery is the recession?
Yes. This is a recession-driven recovery.

That would be pretty unusual, wouldn't it?
We've got scientists coming to Australia to study it. You can't get a hotel in Canberra.

It does sound unusual.
They said it couldn't be done.

Is it a strong recovery?
No, it's not. It's what I would call a weak recovery.

Why is it weak?
It's just being held in check at the moment.

By what?
By the recession.

The recession's not getting any worse, though.
No, it looks a bit like a recovery if you stand in the right position with the light behind it.

How would you describe the recovery?
On the figures available this week, I suppose the recovery is steady without being spectacular.

What does that mean?
It means we're in a recession.

I thought we were over the recession.
Perhaps if we get all the children to hold hands.

Will you be going to assist the Victorian Labor Party in the election campaign?
I'd like to, but unfortunately I can't.

Why not?
Well, we want to get *some* votes.

A Judge of the Late Twentieth Century

I'm not interested in what society thinks.

Thank you for coming in.
Pleasure.

You must have been disturbed by recent indications that members of the judiciary are out of touch on matters of...
Well, I don't think 'out of touch' is the right expression. You'd need to speak to the individual judges involved in these...

Have you spoken to them?
No.

Why not?
I'm not in touch with a great many of them. My point is you'd need to look at the actual cases to see what was said.

What's the problem, do you think?
There's the presumption of innocence. It's a fundamental tenet of our justice system that the accused is presumed innocent. That's all that's happening here. It's steeped in tradition and precedent. There's a famous case, the king and...

Mrs Simpson?
No, the king and...

I?
Look it doesn't matter.

Mr Simpson?
Don't patronise me.

Why not?
That's my job, and by the look of your tie you probably haven't got the Latin.

Why is it that, in cases of rape, the presumption the accused is innocent gets confused with the presumption the victim is guilty?
That sounds very clever, young man, but it isn't the case. Nobody presumes the victim is guilty.

Unless she's married.
Oh, well, they might need a little bit of light sparring if they're married, I think that's fair enough.

What if she says 'yes'?
She's asking for it if she says 'yes'.

What if she says 'no'?
Is she a woman?

Yes.
Very difficult to know what they mean when they say 'no'.

How can it possibly mean anything other than 'no'?
I'd want to have a look at the woman.

Why?
It's none of your bloody business why I want to look at women. I've always liked looking at women.

If you assume a woman is partly responsible for the fact that she is raped, why don't you assume a building is partly responsible for being burgled?
Oh, come on, a building is a building. It has no moral consciousness. It's not a responsible entity.

Why did it get burgled?
Some woman probably left the door open.

Who employs you?
No one employs me. I'm a judge.

Do you have a job?
Yes, I'm a judge.

Who's your employer?
Technically, the attorney-general.

The government. You're a civil servant. Are you telling me you're completely independent of what society thinks?
I'm not interested in what society thinks.

Does the attorney-general provide you with policy guidelines?
Some twelve-year-old with an LLB in geography is going to illuminate the interpretation of the law for us? How very risible.

Who do you listen to?
Sir James, Sir Hamish, Sir Lawrence, Sir William.

Lady Thatcher?
I tell you what, I wouldn't mind getting up there without a ladder. She is all woman...

Thank you.

The Hon. John Hewson
Leader of the Opposition

I'll lead the party in the next election.

Dr Hewson, thanks for joining us.
Pleasure.

Are you a nice man?
Yes, I think I'm a nice man. I think I'm a very nice man.

You seem like a nice man.
Yes, I think I'm a pretty nice man.

Yes.
I don't think you're such a bad bloke either, as a matter of interest.
(They both laugh.)

What do you do in your spare time? What's a typical sort of day for John Hewson?
Well, I don't know that there is such a thing as a typical day.

Oh, touché. You enjoy jogging, I think, don't you?
Yes, I do. I like going for a run.

That's fantastic. A run. You enjoy jogging.
Yes, I get into my running gear and I go for a run.

What would your running gear consist of?
Shoes, shorts and a top.

Are you any good?
I'm not exactly Herb Alpert, but…

Herb Elliot.
(Extends his hand.) John Hewson, Herb. I'm a great admirer of your work.

How do you think you're going at the moment, politically?
I think we're going very well.

You had a ten-point lead in the opinion polls at one stage, didn't you?
Yes, we've got that down to a five-point deficit just with a bit of cost-cutting.

(Bryan speaks into another microphone.) All clear Race Five.
Pardon?

So you'd be pretty pleased with the way things are going at the moment?
I'm delighted with the progress so far this year. It's been a very successful period for both me and…

The Liberal Party?
Yes, it's not going badly for them, either.

(Bryan speaks into another microphone.) Protest Race Six, second against first, alleging interference.
Listen, are you the senior political journalist around here? I'm the leader of the opposition. I get the impression I'm not dealing with the head honcho here.

Yes. You'll be staying on in the leadership for a while?
I'll lead the party in the next election.

Really?
And probably the one after that.

(Bryan speaks into another microphone.) No running near the pool. That boy.
Excuse me?

You'll be the leader, you're saying?
Yes. I've said that.

(Bryan speaks into another microphone.) **That boy running! Get out of the pool!**
Would you mind listening to what I'm saying? Please. This is very important.

(Bryan speaks into another microphone.) **Come in boat number 63, your time is up. What about the election after that?**
Yes, and the one after that.

We're talking about the year 3004.
Yes, I'll still lead the party at that time.

You will lead the party into the March 3004 election? You'll be over a thousand years old.
Listen, pal. I don't care how old I am. I'm going to stay here till I win one.

(Bryan speaks into another microphone.) **Where is boat number 63?**
I've had enough of this. You're not interested in what I've got to say.

I am, Dr Hewson. Can I ask you a question?
Is it sensible?

It's very sensible.
Yes, then.

Did you take out boat number 63?
Yes.

Dr Hewson, I'm afraid your time is up.

The Hon. Jeff Kennett
Premier of Victoria

Have you thanked me for coming in yet?

Mr Kennett, thank you for coming in.
Who are you looking at?

I'm looking at you.
You'll get a bunch of fives up the kisser if you're not careful.

I'm sorry.
That's a good response, son. You're a bit lucky there; you've avoided a nasty incident.

I wonder if I could ask you about your vision for Australia.
I'm Jeff Kennett. I'm the premier of Victoria.

Where do you think Australia's going?
I don't think it's going anywhere, is it? Aren't the other countries coming here? Isn't that the idea?

The Olympics, you're talking about?
It's not just me. Get out there in the streets. Everyone's talking about them. Have you thanked me for coming in yet?

Yes, I did that.
Oh, we've done that, give us a pencil, will you? I'll tick it off.

You've been in office for a while now.
How do you know that?

Mr Kennett, you've been in office for a while now.
Are you looking at me, son?

What have you achieved in that time, do you think?
We lead Australia at the moment. There is no doubt about that. Not a doubt in…

Your mind?
...the whole wide world. This is the only state where anything is
happening.

What is happening, do you think?
The rest of the country is run by honest plodders who are just
scrambling along trying to get the infrastructure to work.

What are you trying to do?
We're crawling around underneath it with a pocketful of gelignite and
a full set of sockets. We're going to fix things.

What are you going to fix?
Education.

What are you going to do?
We're going to stop it.

What's the matter with education?
It's run by teachers. We've got their names. We'll get them.

Didn't you get an education?
No, I went to Scotch—but listen, you can't have an education system
based on the needs of a lot of little children. That doesn't stand to
reason.

**What does the opposition say about all this? Don't you have a bit of
trouble with them?**
Only very occasionally.

There's been complete uproar recently, hasn't there?
Yes, this was over the second reading of the 'My Dad's Bigger Than
Your Dad' bill.

Yes and the 'Nya-Nya-Nya-Nya-Nya' legislation.
We won that.

How did you win it?
Our argument was persuasive.

How?

Eyebrows stuck a frog down someone's trousers.

Wasn't someone suspended?

Yes, but we'll cut him down in the morning and his parents want him to come back next term.

So, more of the same?

A lot of people don't think it's all that sane but, yes, we'll be in there, us Christians.

Mr Kennett, thank you.

You are bloody looking at me, aren't you?

The Hon. Paul Keating
Prime Minister of Australia

A lot of people are interested in clocks.

Mr Keating, thanks for joining us.
Pleasure.

You don't seem to like Alexander Downer very much.
There's nothing personal about my hatred for Mr Downer. I wouldn't want to be misunderstood on this matter.

What? He might be a perfectly nice fellow?
Yes, but I don't think he's representative of the Australian people.

So who does he represent?
A lot of tweedy agrarian plutocrats with tucks sitting around in a hallowed hall getting some wrinkled old retainer to bring them another tray of larks' uvulas. This is not the experience of ordinary people.

And who do you represent?
We represent the ordinary Australians, we're in touch with the lives of ordinary folk.

The ones with the Italian suits?
Yes.

And their abiding interest in English cutlery?
Yes.

Yes, and their knighthoods from Thailand?
Yes.

With the eighteenth-century French chronometers?
I think a lot of people are interested in clocks.

Yes. Chrono's metros, from the Greek.
Well, you can get them from Sotheby's, but you'll need a quid. They cost an arm and a leg.

So I take it you wouldn't agree with the idea that the Labor Party is a bunch of socialists who are taking orders from Moscow?
Come on. Do you think Moscow would have told us to deregulate the financial market? Get the biggest newspaper empire you can find and give it away to a Canadian? Ten per cent unemployment and company profits going up all the time? Do you think the comrades figured that one out? Come on, that argument's not going to work, is it?

So why are you hammering away at them with a lot of old class-war rhetoric from the same period?
This guy is a member of a club fifty per cent of the Australian population can never join. They're just not allowed in.

They're ineligible?
It doesn't matter what they are, pal. They're not allowed to join the outfit. They're not allowed in because they're women. If he is going to mount any pretence to being in some way representative of the Australian people, he should get the rules of that club changed, now.

So that women can join the club?
So that women constitute fifty per cent of the membership of the club. Fifty per cent is the minimum requirement. That's the position we've got. Women as fifty per cent of the Australian community, they should have fifty per cent women members. Not just let them in. Fifty per cent, please.

Change the rules?
Yes, or stop pretending. One or the other.

So you'll be preparing the new legislation over the weekend, will you?
No, no, these people can fix up their own clubs, that's not up to me. I can't do that.

No, I meant the parliament. Fifty per cent women in the parliament. You'll be changing the rules immediately.

In what parliament?

The Australian parliament.

Fifty per cent women in the parliament? *(He looks off.)* Can we have another tray of larks' uvulas, please?

Dr Mahathir Bin Mohamad
Prime Minister of Malaysia

Mr Keating is a very nice man.

Dr Mahathir, thanks for talking to us.
Pleasure.

You have been critical of Australia recently.
I have made some comments about certain things that have been broadcast to the region by Australia.

You've also made some comments about the prime minister, Mr Keating.
Yes, Mr Keating is a very nice man. I saw him this week.

He is a nice man.
Yes, I know I couldn't agree more. I always enjoy talking to him. We have met many times.

What do you talk about?
He tells me Australia's future is in Asia.

And what do you say?
I laugh. He's a very nice man.

Yes, and what do you tell him?
I tell him Malaysia's future is in Canada.

And what does he say?
He laughs. He's a very nice man, Mr Keating. I like him a lot. We get on very well together. I saw him this week.

You don't think Australia's future is in Asia?
I don't know. I am only talking about where Mr Keating says Australia's future is.

He says it's in Asia.
Yes. I like Mr Keating. He's a very nice man.

Yes. Mr Keating is a nice man.
Yes, I'm well aware of that.

What did he say this week?
He told me that taking all the trade barriers and tariffs away would be good for Australia.

And what did you say?
I laughed. He's a very nice man, Mr Keating. I like him.

And what did you tell him?
I told him that for nearly half the year, Malaysia is covered in many hundreds of feet of snow.

And what did he say?
He laughed. He's a very nice man, Mr Keating. I do like him.

Did he tell you that Australia might extend its free-trade arrangements to other countries?
To countries other than where its future is?

Yes.
Yes. He's a very nice man, Mr Keating. I like him a lot.

What did you say?
I told him the one about the Princess and the Frog.

And what did he say?
He told me Australia would have the right to put the tariffs up again if it wanted to.

And what did you say?
I laughed. He's a great fellow, Mr Keating. I like him.

Will you be seeing him again soon?
Yes, I hope so.

When?
Well, I'm back in Malaysia now, dealing with reality.

And then you'll be seeing Mr Keating again?
Oh yes. I like Mr Keating. He's a very nice man.

Yes, we like him, too.
Yes, I know that.

How do you know that?
He told me.

And what did you say?
I laughed. He's a very nice man, Mr Keating. We get on very well. He's a marvellous fellow.

He is, isn't he?
Oh yes. I enjoy him enormously.

The Hon. Alexander Downer
Leader of the Opposition

Let's not talk about the republic.

Mr Downer, thanks for coming in.
Pleasure. You don't want to talk about the republic do you?

Yes, I do really. Why?
Let's not talk about the republic. I've been doing it all week.

Hang on, Mr Downer. This is the major political issue confronting this country.
What about the government decision against worm-rot? There are plenty of other things to talk about.

Like what?
I've just listed some of them. There are plenty of them.

You mentioned the government decision against worm-rot.
There's another one. There are tons of them.

Why don't you want to talk about the republic?
Because I've got to argue against it.

But you are against it, aren't you?
Who watches this program? Have you got the demographics there?

Yes. (Indicates piece of paper.)
Let me see. (*Looks at the piece of paper.*) Oh yes, I am totally against a republic.

But of course some of those older people will have gone to bed by now.
In that case I favour the republic.

You support the idea of Australia's becoming a republic.
Well, I'm forty-three; I'm a bit caught here. A lot of my parents'
generation are quite upset by all this republican talk and a lot of
younger people think differently. Now, obviously I can't talk to them
both at the same time.

Sure you can.
Well, I'd like to say to the older people in the Liberal Party that Mr Keating wants to do away with the Queen and install some grubby little left-wing system of his own because, of course, he wants more power. He's got no respect for the traditions of Australia's long-standing and very honorable connection with the British royal family. All stand please now for the anthem. *(Sings 'God Save the Queen'.)*

Now, you younger people. Gidday. I'm Alexander Downer, the funky new head of the opposition, the dangerous bunch of radicals who are against the government. We inhale but we don't smoke. This is your future we're talking about here and it's very important that you know what's going to happen. There's going to be a referendum and you'll all get to vote about whether or not we want our head of state to be somebody from another country, or whether we want to be independent and responsible for our own destiny. Think about it. Cowabunga, dudes. *(Sings the French national anthem.)*

What do you really think?
I think it's inevitable.

You think we're going to become a republic. Why don't you come out in favour of it?
I'll lose the party. I can't afford to do that.

But you're not a monarchist. Why did you come out against a republic?
Well, look. There's a bigger issue. Who's going to run a republic?
That's my concern. We don't want Mr Keating running the republic.

Why not?
You can't trust him.

Why not?
He tricked me into supporting a monarchy and I'm a republican. And I'm the leader of the opposition. What chance have ordinary people got?

The Hon. John Howard
Leader of the Opposition
I just had a déjà vu.

Mr Howard, thanks for coming in.
Oh, thank you very much and good evening.

And congratulations on becoming the new leader.
Thank you very much. Have we had this conversation before?

No, I don't think so.
No, that's all right. I just had a déjà vu.

No, I don't think so.
No, that's OK. I just had a déjà vu.

No, I don't think so.
No, it's OK. I just had a déjà vu.

How do you think I feel?
We've never had this conversation before?

No, I don't think so.
You've never said that to me before?

No, I don't think so.
Yes.

No, I don't think so.
That's very, very strange. I just had a...

Déjà vu?
You're having a déjà vu?

No, I don't think so.
Is this happening now?

Yes, of course it is.
This conversation, are we talking now? Are we actually talking now?

Yes.
This is not something we're doing in the past?

No, I just congratulated you on becoming leader of the opposition.
This is very, very weird. This is very weird. You're telling me we've never had this conversation before?

No, I don't think so.
It's very, very odd. It's very strange.

Well, there were no other candidates.
No candidates? Where was Andrew?

Andrew Peacock?
Yes.

He's resigned. He's retired.
Retired? Can I ask you a personal question?

Sure.
What year is it?

It's 1995.
Oh my God! Oh, this is terribly, terribly strange.

Look, Mr Howard, Mr Downer was the leader. You replaced him, and you're now leader of the opposition.
Alexander Downer?

Yes.
Alexander Downer was leader of the Liberal Party?

Yes.
Was I loyal to him?

A hundred per cent.
I bet I was not. Who's my deputy now?

Peter Costello.

Good grief. Peter? What's the current account deficit?

Twenty-five billion.

Well, why don't we put interest rates up?

Oh no.

What's the trouble?

Oh, that's weird.

What's the matter?

I just had a déjà vu.

There'll be some unemployment, but who gives a stuff? You can't stop that anyway.

Wow, that's weird. I just had a déjà vu.

Really? I'll tell you the real problem in this country. I'll tell you the real problem in this country.

Immigration.

Immigration.

Wow, that is really weird.

Are you OK?

I just had a déjà vu.

Hang on, I'll get you a glass of water.

That's mega-weird.

Hang on, I've got you a glass of water before. We've done this be…
Have we been here…We've…been…Ray!

Mr Solomon Lew
Chairman, Coles Myer Ltd

We sell this interview back to the network.

Mr Lew, thanks for coming in.
Pleasure.

I wonder if I can ask you about the events that have led up to the events of this week?
The events of last week led to the events of this week.

No, the whole thing. The whole build-up. There are allegations about the way that this board has operated, aren't there? There have been for some time.
Yes. Can I make a suggestion?

Yes.
This is an important interview. The network wants it?

Yes.
I haven't spoken to anyone else.

No.
I mean, the phone has been running red-hot, but this is the only one I'm doing.

We're very grateful.
Yes, they'll want this interview.

They do. They're mad keen.
OK. Now, you and I form a company.

We do what?
Which is owned by other companies we own.

I don't own any companies.
We'll get you one. They cost sixpence. Trust me.

But why?
And we sell this interview back to the network.

But I already work for the network.
Yes, but your company doesn't, and I don't.

But you don't need to, you've got $500 million.
How do you think I got it? Trust me. And we deliver the interview to the network.

But the network is already employing me. Why would they pay me to do something I'm already doing?
So it could all be done efficiently. It'll be efficient. We get rid of these chairs.

What's the matter with the chairs?
We don't like them. They're no good.

They look all right to me.
No, we need new ones.

Where do we get new chairs?
From our chair supply company.

We supply chairs?
We've got an interview requisites supply company. We supply everything. Lights, cameras, recorders.

But all this stuff is already here.
Yes, but it's more efficient this way.

But that'll cost a fortune.
Well, do they want the interview or don't they? If they want us, they have to buy the package that contains us.

What if the people paying found out?
Plan B.

What's plan B?
Get someone who can talk for an hour and a half without saying anything to go out and make an announcement.

What would Mr Greiner say?
He wouldn't say anything. 'Time of healing.' 'Full investigation.'

'Vigorous investigation.'
'Vigorous.' 'Characterised by its extreme vigour.'

'Traumatic time for the company.'
'Problems of perception' and so on, yes.

Will it work, do you reckon?
One of us might have to resign.

Which one?
The one who isn't your partner, ideally.

Business as usual.
Say goodnight.

Why?
We're supplying 'goodnight', as a concept, to the network.

Thanks for coming in.
Yes, we do that one, too.

We'll have to leave it there, thanks.
Yes, we're killing them.

We're out of time.
Wow! We're cooking!

The Howard Apology

11 March 1996 – 3 December 2007

Mr Howard, thanks for joining us.
Pleasure.

It must have been the biggest buzz. Did you ever think you'd win an Oscar?
No.

It was a good role?
Dream role: little guy, typical of his time, confused, slightly peculiar.

How is he confused?
Well, he's supposed to be a leader and he doesn't do any leading. He has a kind of psychological crisis. He can't decide what to do.

Who is he supposed to be leading?
Well, he has got himself into the position at one stage where he's running an entire country.

So what does he do?
Oh, you'll have to see the film.

The Hon. Jeff Kennett
Premier of Victoria

How dare you turn up in a jacket in that condition.

Mr Kennett, thanks for coming in.
Permission to speak?

Permission to speak, sir?
Watch it.

Mr Kennett, these shares you bought...
I didn't buy any shares.

Your wife bought them.
Yes, what about them?

Why did she buy them?
My wife has always had an interest in Chinese building-supply companies.

Is she interested in Chinese building materials generally?
Can I speak frankly?

Yes.
She speaks of little else.

She has bought rather a lot of them.
She didn't get as many as she wanted.

Yes, but she got 50,000.
As I said, she has an abiding interest in Chinese building-supply companies.

She sold about 30,000 of them later, didn't she? Why?
I would imagine it's difficult to remain interested in Chinese building materials for very lengthy periods.

When she sold them, had the price gone up?
What do you mean 'up'?

As distinct from down.
Are you suggesting that my wife should have taken a bath on a share transaction because I'm the premier? Is that what you're suggesting?

Mr Kennett, do you think you're too closely connected with business?
Oh, I think if either of them had a problem, I'd have heard about it by now.

Either who?
Well, who are you talking about?

The people of Victoria.
Look, I see them both regularly and neither of them has ever suggested there might be a problem.

The Grand Prix was a huge success.
Huge success. Huge success. Good for Victoria. Melbourne was seen on television in 127 million countries.

One hundred and twenty-seven million countries?
Are you questioning me?

No.
Good.

Did it make money?
It made millions. Don't you read the paper?

Why did it run at a loss?
That's just an accounting exercise. We'll sack some teachers or something. Those buttons are a disgrace.

Pardon?
How dare you turn up with a jacket in that condition. That's a disgrace. Am I hurting you, soldier?

No.
I should be. I'm standing on your hair.

Standing on my hair?
Get a haircut.

Mr Kennett.
Permission to speak.

Permission to speak, sir.
Shut up. Ten push-ups.

Pardon?
I said shut up. Ten push-ups, get on with it.

You want me to do ten push-ups?
I'll stick you on a charge in a minute, son. Do as you're told.

Mr Kennett, I just wanted to ask some questions about the way things are going in Victoria.
Right. That's it. Get up. Come on. Outside.
(They go outside, Bryan protesting.)

Mr Kennett, all I want to do is ask you some questions about the way you run things.
Don't you worry about that, you horrible little Christian. Out here.
Now, twice around the compound.

What do you mean, 'twice around the compound'?
Put the pack on. Twice around. Move it. Soldier. *(A guard comes over.)*
Keep this man covered.

Where are you going?
None of your business. Shut up. *(To camera.)* Carry on!

Senator Robert Hill
Minister for the Environment

It's a constant, the environment.

Senator Hill, thanks for your time.
Pleasure.

What are you going to do if you can't get the sale of Telstra through the senate?
We will.

What will you do if you don't?
We will.

What will you do if you don't?
We'll have to think of another way of doing it.

Doing what?
Selling Telstra.

What about the environment?
It will still be there. It's a constant, the environment.

What about environmental policy?
We won't have one.

Why not?
We won't bother about the environment if we don't sell Telstra.

Do you mean we won't care about it?
We won't bother about it. We won't be able to.

Why not?
We won't have the money to do it.

Won't the environmental problems still exist?
What environmental problems?

Global warming. The hole in the ozone layer. Emission controls.
Never heard of them. What's your question?

What are you going to do about them?
Sell Telstra.

What if you can't?
We won't do anything about them.

Do you have any plan for funding environmental policies other than selling Telstra?
No.

So what is your environmental policy?
To sell Telstra.

What's your portfolio?
Minister for the environment.

And what's your job?
To sell Telstra.

And what if you can't?
Maybe we'll have a new minister for the...

Environment?
Yes.

What will that person's job be?
Sell Telstra.

But that's not an environmental policy.
Yes, it is. I'm the minister for the environment and that is my job.

I give up.
Good lad. They said you would.

Thanks for your time.
Can you lend me forty cents?

What for?
I want to make a quick environmental policy.

The Hon. Alexander Downer
Minister for Foreign Affairs

I didn't tell a porkie.

Mr Downer, thanks for your time.
Pleasure.

You misled the parliament this week. You told a porkie.
No, I didn't tell a porkie. I misled the parliament by providing it with information which I thought, at the time I gave it, was correct.

Of course. And you apologised?
Yes.

What for?
For telling porkies.

What was it about? What had you done?
I had decided to cut a whole lot of aid projects in Asia and I said the government had received no complaints or expressions of concern about this.

And had anyone expressed concern?
As it happened, when I thought about it, we had had one or two mentions made of it.

What do you mean mentions?
Well, casual references made to it in conversations about something else.

Like what?
Like 'Dear Mr Downer, congratulations on becoming Australia's foreign minister, we're extremely concerned that you might be stopping the aid scheme.'

What was the main point of that letter?
To congratulate me on becoming foreign minister.

You're good aren't you?
Well, I'm keen.

So when you said no one had complained, who had actually said anything?
These people. *(He holds up a 400-page printout.)*

Who are they?
The undersecretary for international trade in the Philippines.

Where are the Philippines?
I don't know. Up there somewhere.

(He shows Mr Downer on a map.) **Here they are.**
Oh, I've flown over them a thousand times.

Next?
China.

China?
Someone from China was upset.

Do we trade with China?
We used to.

When?
Till Thursday we did. They were quite a big trading partner of ours.

Where is China?
Near the Soviet Union.

I can't find the Soviet Union.
Bounded by China and the Ottoman Empire.

Ottoman Empire?
Yes. It's near Gaul.

Gaul?
Can you find Kent? It's near Kent. I could *drive* there from Kent.

Kent.

Hey, there's a picture of me on that map.

Where?

That looks like me, there, up in the corner.

No, he's just a little man who blows the wind.

He does look like me though, doesn't he? I like him.

The Hon. Bob Carr
Premier of New South Wales

I want to change the anthem.

Mr Carr, thanks for coming in.
Pleasure.

You want to change the national anthem?
I want to change the anthem that presents Australia to the world in Sydney in 2000.

From 'Advance Australia Fair'?
Yes.

What's the matter with 'Advance Australia Fair'?
It doesn't represent us. It's a nineteenth-century madrigal. It sounds like Tennyson.

Tennis and what?
No, Tennyson. Alfred Tennyson.

The poet?
Yes.

You mean it's old-fashioned?
Yes, 'Girt by Sea'.

Who's she?
Gert?

Yes.
I don't know.

A woman on a beach somewhere.
A friend of the poet perhaps, but who cares? It's not relevant.

OK. Why 'Waltzing Matilda'?
Well, it speaks of who we are.

We're sheep-stealers?
No, but we're bushmen.

Are you a bushman, Mr Carr?
I'm frankly, personally, not a bushman, no, but you know what I mean. You can smell the wattle in the song, ya da dada da. What Australian heart doesn't leap?

But we're not like that. Sydney certainly isn't like that.
We can adapt it.

So that it reflects the way we are now?
Yes, easy.

How?
Well, 'Once a joint with every advantage.'

'Destroyed its education system.'
No. I was thinking, 'Full of young and vigorous citizens.'

That's catchy.
Well, 'healthy citizens'. 'Full of young and healthy citizens.'

Except the Aborigines. Aboriginal health is a scandal. The UN is looking at what we're doing there.
And what are we doing?

Cutting the budget.
Well, 'full of young and healthy white citizens. Under the shade...'

The 'shame'.
'Shame'? Why?

You want it to reflect the current position?
Yes.

'Under the shame.'
'Under the shame of a...'

'…lying politician.'

Actually, where are we going to broadcast this?

Well, it's the people's song.

Yes, good point, a very good point. We'll stick it out on the AB—

On the what?

Doesn't matter, why bother?

Mr Carr, thank you.

I don't know why I bother.

The Hon. John Howard
Prime Minister of Australia

This is my pen.

Mr Howard, thanks for coming in.
Hang on, I'm not quite ready.

I'd just like to talk to you about the Wik decision.
Hang on. I'll be with you in a minute.

You're going to extinguish Native Title, aren't you?
Whoops, good grief. Hang on, I'm sitting on something.
What's this thing?

Oh I'm sorry, that's my pen.
It's yours?

Yes. I must have left it there.
I think this is mine, isn't it?

Can I have a look? No, that's mine.
I just sat on it.

Yes, but it's my pen.
It's yours?

Yes.
Why aren't you using it, if it's yours?

What do you mean 'using it'? It's my pen.
You're not using it.

I don't need it at the moment, Mr Howard. I'm talking to you.
Well, you don't need it, then. I'll have it.

I'll need it later.
OK, I need it now. I'll have it.

Look, you can use it.
You want me to use it?

Yes, that's OK. You can use it. We can both use it.
We can both use it?

Yes.
OK. It'll be mine then.

Why is it yours because we both want to use it? You're not using it now.
Yes, I am, look at this. *(He writes.)* 'This is my pen. It is nice.' I'm writing, look at this. There's writing coming out the end of it.

That's not what it's for.
Not what it's for? Of course, it's what it's for. What else can you do with a pen?

Do drawings.
You do drawings with it?

Yes.
Writing's more important than drawing. I'll keep it.

No, it's not. I've always done drawings with it.
Yes, it is. Writing's more important than drawing. I'll keep the pen. That's settled. What was your question? Wik? Native Title?

What if I want to do drawings?
Well, you don't, do you? You've just said you wanted to talk to me.

Why can't we share the pen?
No. Too much uncertainty.

What do you mean 'uncertainty'?
Well, I wouldn't own it that way, would I?

Why should you own it? It's my pen.
We've just been through that. I want to use it, you're not using it at the moment. I'll have it, thank you. Let's get on with it.

Why can't we both use it?
Why do you want it at all? You're not using it.

It belonged to my grandfather.
All right, I'll give you a couple of bucks for it.

Hang on. Mr Howard, I'm not interested in the money. Surely we can both use the pen. You want to write with it, I want to do drawings. What's the problem?
Too much uncertainty.

Why do you keep saying there's uncertainty?
Listen, I don't want to hear a lot of drivel about some mystical semi-religious historical connection with the pen. I need to use the thing.

I need it too, Mr Howard.
To do drawings?

Yes.
What do you do for a living, son?

I do drawings.
Well, you can get another job can't you?

Where? What other job?
Can't you get a job writing?

No. Why should everybody have to get a job writing?
Why can't you get a job writing? What's the matter with you? Is there something wrong with you?

Mr Howard, what I do is drawings.
You're bloody hopeless I reckon, you people, you're bloody hopeless.

Mr Howard, it would be quite easy to share the pen.
No, it wouldn't.

Why not?
Because I'm not going to bloody do it, that's why.

On what legal basis can you make that claim?
Do you speak Latin?

Yes.
Finders Keepers.

Mr Howard, that pen is important to me. It's part of my heritage.
It's part of mine, too.

It belonged to my grandfather.
I'm going to give it to my grandson.

I don't see why we can't share it.
Too much uncertainty. We've been through all that. What did you want to ask me about?

I was going to ask you about extinguishing Native Title.
Oh, shut up. I'm sick of you.

Mr Howard, thank you for coming in.

The Hon. John Howard
Prime Minister of Australia

Yes, but…

Mr Howard, thanks for coming in.
Pleasure.

I wonder if I could ask you: do you think Australians are racist?
No, I don't, but (oh blast, I've got to stop doing that).

What's the problem?
I keep sticking a 'but' at the end of my sentences. I must try to stop doing that.

Do you think you can stop doing it?
Well, I'd like to think so, but…

What's the problem with saying 'but' at the end of everything you say?
Well, it undermines everything you've just said. You can say something perfectly reasonable. You can say what you meant to say. You can say what you think is appropriate.

You can say what you know very well you ought to say.
Yes, but (bugger it).

As prime minister, I suppose sometimes you've also got to say what you think the people of Australia would want you to say.
Yes…

Careful.
…but (blast).

Have you tried just not saying anything?
Yes, but…

But you can't.
No, I can't. Some people are good at being brief, at saying just enough, at judging exactly how much to say and stopping there.

Some people are quite good at expressing themselves.
Yes, they are, but...

But you're not one of them.
Yes, I am, but...

Don't you have speech writers?
Yes, I do, but...

Was this the problem in Melbourne at the Reconciliation Convention?
No. There's another problem there. We've got to get the people who are going to Pauline Hanson concerts to come back to the Coalition.

Do you agree with what Pauline Hanson is saying?
No, but (blast).

Why don't you speak against her?
I do...

Watch out.
...but...

Mr Howard. What were you being asked to apologise for?
To the Aborigines.

Yes.
For a whole lot of things that have been happening to them for the last 200 years.

Since we got here.
Yes, but we didn't do it.

Look, I might be able to help you out here. These things that have happened to the Aboriginal people. What were they?
Oh, it varies. It's not even the same in each case. In some areas they were wiped out. In some places they had their land taken away from them. In some cases we gave them diseases. In some cases they had their children taken off them.

Did all these things happen?
Yes, of course they did. But I didn't do them.

Hang on. Did it happen? Forget about who did it. Did it happen?
Yes, it did, but I repeat, I didn't do it and neither did Pauline Hanson.

Mr Howard, didn't you just have to express the view that you were sorry it had happened?
Yes, but...

It doesn't seem impossible, does it?
It's all right for you. You're not speaking from where I was speaking at the time.

Where were you talking from?
But.

You were talking out your butt?
Oh, God. Now *you've* got it.

The Hon. Philip Ruddock
Minister for Immigration

You can't come into Australia if you're not an immigrant.

Mr Ruddock, thanks for joining us.
Pleasure.

I'd like to ask you about this decision to reduce immigration.
Only by immigrants.

Pardon?
We're only cutting down on the number of *immigrants* who can come into the country.

From overseas.
We believe that's where they're coming from, in the main, yes.

So other than immigrants, anyone can come?
No, no one else can come. I haven't made myself clear. You can't come into Australia if you're not an immigrant. You've got to be an immigrant to get in. That's what an immigrant is.

So you can't come at all if you're not an immigrant.
That's right.

And you're cutting down on the number who can come because they are immigrants.
Well, they won't be immigrants now because we're not going to let them in.

No, but they'd be immigrants if you'd let them come here.
No, they'd be Australians if we let them come in, but we're not going to.

Mr Ruddock, you're not making sense.
How dare you. I'm the minister for...

Letting people in.
Keeping people out.

Who are you letting in?
Well, we let you in.

I was born here.
We're not preventing people who were born here from coming in.
You've got nothing to worry about.

Why would you prevent people who were born here from coming in?
Yes. That was our feeling. *(He is suddenly distracted and speaks in an urgent whisper.)* Is that Pauline Hanson? In the other studio. Hello Pauline.

Mr Ruddock.
It is. It's Pauline Hanson. Stand up.

Pardon?
Have some respect. Get up.

Mr Ruddock. You say this decision has got nothing to do with Pauline Hanson.
Nothing whatever, no. Hello there.

What are you going to do next?
Don't know. I don't know what she's saying. See if we can find out what she's saying. You never know what she's going to say.

Why do you need to know what she's saying?
So we can make a decision that's got nothing to do with that either.

Do you agree with what Pauline Hanson is saying?
I don't know what she is saying. I can't hear her.

Do you agree with what she's saying generally?
No I don't. Certainly not. Hello Pauline. Philip Ruddock, Canberra.

Well, why don't you make a stand against her?
Because I don't wish to dignify her comments by entering into a discussion with her. I've met her you know. I've actually met Pauline Hanson.

If you don't want to help her, why are you waiting to see what she says before you make your next policy announcement?
So that we as a government can continue to be completely uninfluenced by her unrepresentative, poisonous, racist policies. Oh, she's looking over here. Look at that. She recognises me. Philip Ruddock. Good morning.

She's writing something for you. She's going to hold it up.
No, I can't send Aborigines out, dear. I'm only in charge of who's coming in. I'm sorry, I can't. Yes, I agree with you dear, but…

You said you didn't.
Shut up, I'm talking to the prime minister.

The Hon. John Howard
Prime Minister of Australia

It was the magic of the guy himself.

Mr Howard, thanks for joining us.
Pleasure.

Have you calmed down yet?
I'm getting used to it a bit now, yes.

It must just have been the biggest buzz. Did you ever think you'd win an Oscar?
No.

I mean you couldn't really have, I suppose.
Oh, you don't dare to hope, no.

It was a good role.
Dream role.

How did you get it?
Well, I wanted it.

You lobbied for it?
Oh yes, I went after it with a big stick.

Why?
I knew it was the part for me. Made in heaven.

OK, why was this one the one?
Well, I think it was the magic of the guy himself; little guy, typical of his time, confused, slightly peculiar.

Talks to himself.
Pardon?

He talks to himself.
Yes, they both do.

How is he confused?
Well, he's supposed to be a leader and he doesn't do any leading. Have you seen the film?

No, not yet.
Have a look when you see the film. He's immobilised. He can't do it.

Why not?
He has a kind of psychological crisis. He can't decide what to do.

Who is he supposed to be leading?
Well, he's got himself into the position at one stage where he's running an entire country.

Oh dear. And he doesn't know what he's doing?
Hasn't got a clue. There's some suggestion it's all to do with his father.

So what does he do?
Oh, you'll have to see the film.

Well, what sort of thing does he do?
For example, he lets a woman in Queensland run it for a while.

Is that a good idea?
Well, you know the tourist industry?

Yes.
That takes care of that.

Why does he do that?
Well, he's having this psychological crisis. It's easy to be critical. Have some compassion, please.

OK. What does he do after that? Are we up to Wik 3 yet?
I don't know what Wik it was. It was fairly early on.

Is it still on?
Yes, it's on for young and old now. It's getting worse.

I mean the film.
What film?

Mr Howard, thanks for joining us.
Could I just thank Paul, Pauline and poor people generally.

Mr Howard. Take a bow.
I'll be right. I'll one up on the way out.

The Hon. Kim Beazley
Leader of the Opposition

At least we didn't win it.

Mr Beazley, thanks for your time.
Good to see you, Bryan.

Had a good year?
I've had a very good year, yes. Enjoyed it a lot.

Lost an election?
Lost an election, yes, but at least we didn't win it.

That wouldn't have been good?
No, we'd be running the country now if we'd won it.

Didn't you want to run the country?
Ooh, no. Bad business, running the country.

You said you did before the election.
Well, you've got to say you want to run the country if you're standing in an election.

You'd have to say that, I suppose.
Yes, there's not much point in saying, 'Vote for us, we bat down to about number three and we've got the same policies as the other lot.'

Of course not. 'Vote for us, we don't want to be the government.'
No, you can't say that.

People wouldn't vote for you, would they?
No, they wouldn't. And they didn't.

It worked.
That's right. It was a completely successful campaign.

So what's next for you?
More of the same. We'll be opposing. The job of an opposition is to oppose.

But you're not opposing the people who run the country, are you?
Oh no, we're not crazy, there's no future in that. You're not going to get anywhere opposing the people who are actually in power.

Why not?
They're the popular ones. They're the ones with the public support.

So who are you opposing?
We're opposing the government.

How do you do that if you're not really opposed to what they're doing?
Well, you say you're opposed to what they're doing.

Can you give me an example?
Yes. You say, 'We are opposed to all this economic rationalism.'

Because it has tossed hundreds of thousands of people out of work?
Yes. It exports jobs. Shifts control of the economy outside the country.

Removes the checks and balances?
It does. And it forces society to cannibalise itself.

You say all those things?
Yes.

But your policies don't depart much from economic rationalism.
No, they can't afford to.

Why not?
The people who run things might get annoyed.

Would they say so?
Oh, yes. You'd know all about it.

How?

The dollar would get a shagging. You wouldn't be able to afford a fridge or a lawnmower.

Society would fall apart.

It would be the end of the Westinghouse system.

Westminster system.

I beg your pardon. I used to know all this stuff.

You think we're seeing the collapse of the Westminster system?

I think under the Howard miracle, you won't even be able to get the parts...

Thanks for your time.

...but don't tell anyone I said that.

The Hon. John Howard
Prime Minister of Australia

I explained that I was in a spot of bother.

Mr Howard, thanks for your time.
Pleasure.

You've been meeting with Meg Lees almost every day since we last spoke.
I have, yes.

And how has it gone?
Very well. What a nice person.

She is a nice person, isn't she?
It was most enjoyable.

What actually happened?
We sat down. We spoke in a general manner.

What did you say to her?
I explained that I was in a spot of bother. Needed a bit of a hand.

A bit of advice?
Yes. I ran it past her in broad outline.

How did you describe the problem?
I said I was running a democracy.

What did she say?
I tell you what, she's got a very good sense of humour.

Likes a laugh?
Oh, she's wicked.

Did you actually say you were running a democracy?
Yes.

Don't the people run a democracy?
And you reckon she didn't pick *that* up?

She's quick.
Doesn't miss a trick.

Did you explain what you'd done?
Yes. She asked me for a bit more information.

What did you tell her?
I said I'd brought in a policy people didn't want, without consulting them on the detail. And without having the numbers in the parliament.

Is this conversation recorded?
Yes. It's all official. There are minutes and so on.

Are there?
Yes. It's like Hansard. Here are the minutes from yesterday, I was just checking through them.

Can I have a look?
I don't see why not. I'm planning to be out of the country when the tax comes in.

(He reads.) 'The meeting began at 10.22.'
It's good, isn't it? What does it say next?

'Mr Howard asked Meg Lees whether she had considered his offer.'
That's right.

'Ms Lees asked whether this was the same offer he had made a week previously and which had been rejected on approximately 312 separate occasions.'
'Mr Howard sought some guidance as to the precise number of times it was necessary to repeat a statement in fairly simple English in order for its delivery to be effective.'

'**Ms Lees requested clarification as to whether or not perhaps there was some flannel or heavy towelling material impeding the passage of sound through Mr Howard's aural passages.**'
'There was some speculation from Mr Howard as to Ms Lees' apparent incapacity to distinguish between the lower reaches of her torso and her elbow.'

'**Ms Lees suggested a brief adjournment at this point which would provide Mr Howard with an opportunity to see an ophthalmologist.**'
'In an attempt to break the deadlock Mr Howard ventured the opinion that it might be an excellent idea if Ms Lees were to avail herself of the education system and in particular the aspects of it whose job it is to accentuate the knowledge of the broader public in the area of economics.'

'**Ms Lees asserted that this was a privilege already vouchsafed to her and she expressed some surprise that a detailed knowledge of macroeconomic reform in its many aspects was a part of the training normally available to small-minded suburban solicitors.**'
'Mr Howard asked whether or not there was any point in continuing with this conversation, richly-textured and enlightening though it undoubtedly was.'

'**Ms Lees concurred and suggested that should Mr Howard have a brief period over the next couple of hours when he wasn't being instructed what to do by big business or Treasury, he might like to go out into the street and see how much photochemical smog was being produced by diesel engines.**'
'Mr Howard attempted to disavow Ms Lees of the view that he had arrived in conjunction with the previous shower.'

'**Ms Lees named a prominent religious figure and offered a detailed suggestion about the exact placement of the GST as outlined.**'
'It was agreed that the meeting would reconvene after lunch.'

What's this here about food?

That's just a note to myself, for our next meeting, to make sure we've got something to eat.

Why?

All through the meeting she wanted to get takeaway food.

Really?

Yes. Takeout food. She kept saying it over and over.

The Hon. Tim Fischer
Leader of the National Country Party

My watch is in the glovebox.

Tim Fischer, thanks for your time.
Good to talk to you, Bryan.

You must have been pleased with the response to your decision to get out of politics.
Yes. I have been affected by the warmth of the response, yes, both from colleagues.

And from who else?
No. They were both from colleagues from memory.

You're being given a fair old send-off in the media, aren't you?
There are some very fine journalists in Australia. I think it's one of the things we do best.

Let's go back over some of the events of your time in politics, because it's been an interesting time, hasn't it?
It has. I wouldn't have missed it for quids.

You were elected in…what?
I was elected in New South Wales.

Yes. What year?
1999.

So how long were you in there?
I've got no idea. My watch is in the glovebox.

No, I'm asking about the period since you were first elected into parliament.
Oh yes, you're not allowed in if you're not elected, that's the way it works.

When was that?
Yes, no doubt about that at all.

Just reading from tomorrow's paper here...
I'm in tomorrow's paper?

There's very little else in it. It's mostly you, tomorrow's paper.
Did they use the photos?

Yes, here you are in the army...
Yes, that's me.

What's this here? This is you being a statesman, is it?
No, I'm just wearing a hat.

It says here 'Tim Fischer: The Statesman'.
That must be the car. I'm just standing there in a hat.

Here you are splitting the atom.
No, I'm just wearing a hat again. Here I am going for a swim, look.
That's up the bush.

Yes, 'Tim Fischer: The Great Australian' it says here.
Great Australian?

Yes.
That can't be right. I voted for a GST.

Here's one of you with a store dummy.
Where?

Here. You're showing an R. M. Williams store dummy a sheep.
That's John Howard.

No. That's a sheep.
This other one here. That's John Howard.

What's he looking like that for?
He's trying to look like an Australian.

Why?
He's going to bring in a GST.

Will you miss the cut and thrust? Do you think?
Two questions there.

Let's take the first one. Will you miss the cut and thrust?
No. I'm getting out before they introduce a GST.

But you helped bring it in.
Exactly. I'm not a complete idiot.

Well, what's this then?
That's me in the hat again.

Mr Fischer, thanks for your time.
Gidday. I'm Tim Fischer. How are you?

Senator Robert Hill
Minister for the Environment

Australian industry at work.

Senator Hill, thanks for your time.
Very good to be here.

You must be pleased.
Yes, indeed.

To have Kakadu listed as a uranium mine.
It's a great result. We're very proud.

Good for Australia.
Australia didn't do it. *We* did it.

I mean it's good for Australia that it happened.
You've lost me.

Is it tough to get a site listed as a uranium mine?
Yes, it's quite a detailed process.

How do you do it?
First of all you've got to get elected.

How do you do that?
You adopt a lot of policies you think people will like.

Like what?
Like envirotuninal policies.

Environmental policies?
That's them.

You're the minister for the environment.
Of course I am. I just turned part of it into a uranium mine.

So you get into power with your environmental policies. And then what do you do?
You do what you like once you're in.

This is why we're increasing greenhouse gases?
Yes.

And turning a national park into a uranium mine?
Not the whole park.

A park with a uranium mine in it?
Yes. Nice big park. Few trees. Shrubs. Herbaceous borders.

And a uranium mine.
Australian industry at work.

You won't be able to drink the water.
Why not?

It'll be poisoned. That's what happens with a uranium mine.
The miners will take the water with them.

Is it a beautiful place?
Not really. It's a big hole in the ground full of trucks and bulldozers.

I mean Kakadu.
Kakadu? It is now, yes.

You don't think it always will be?
We've given an international undertaking to turn it into a uranium mine.

You've promised?
Solemnly.

Mr Hill, thanks for your time.
This is a Howard government promise.

The Hon. John Howard
Prime Minister of Australia

The UN has got no business criticising us at all.

Mr Howard, thanks for your time.
Good evening, very good to be with you.

Mr Howard, how many policies do you have on Aboriginal affairs?
Do you mean in town or in the bush?

Let's look at the 'in town' ones first.
In the city, or in the regional centres?

In the cities.
In an election year or just normally?

All the time, ideally.
An all-the-time, work-for-all-cases Aboriginal policy?

Yes.
I'm afraid I don't understand your question.

Let me put it this way. Can you explain the business of mandatory sentencing?
Certainly. Do you know what mandatory sentencing is?

No, that's what I want to ask you.
OK. Do you know what 'mandatory' means?

It means obligatory.
What does obligatory mean?

Obligatory?
Is it Irish?

Not O'Bligatory. Obligatory.
Where is it? Is it up in the Territory?

It's a bit like 'unavoidable'.
Ah yes. Mighty pretty country round there. I was up there recently.

You were in the Northern Territory?
No, but I was up that way.

Where were you?
I had to go up to Pymble for a meeting.

Mr Howard, why is the United Nations being critical of Australia at the moment?
I don't know. I've been trying to work that out. This has got nothing to do with the United Nations.

What hasn't?
The treatment of Aboriginal people in Australia.

The UN has said they haven't got basic human rights.
The UN has got no business criticising us at all.

Why not?
Because we support them. We helped write their human rights charter.

They have a human rights charter?
Yes, the member countries of the United Nations formed a charter years ago.

Are we a member of the UN?
A very important member. Doc Evatt wrote a fair bit of the UN charter.

And what is the purpose of the UN human rights policy?
To prevent governments from acting in a way which would threaten the lives of their own citizens.

Would that happen?
It has. Look at East Timor.

That was tragic, wasn't it?
Sometimes a government is so bad, so bereft of what the broader world would accept as a basic standard of moral responsibility to its own citizens...

...that it will simply ignore the plight and condition of sections of its own people?
Yes.

And what might happen?
Many of them will die.

So the UN seeks to protect the fundamental human rights of those people?
That's the idea.

And if it doesn't, who will?
Exactly. If the UN doesn't say something about the condition of these people, their privations and their distress might continue.

These are genuinely appalling governments you're talking about, aren't they?
They are. I'm citing the extreme to highlight the UN policy and its importance.

So what is our objection to the UN's criticism of us on this issue?
It's none of their business when it happens here in Australia.

Do you mean 'What right do they have to speak about what's going on in an individual country?'
I do. We're running Australia. The United Nations isn't running a country.

Doesn't it represent all the countries?
Yes, but there's a difference between what you'd like to happen and what actually happens in the real world. It's like going to church. You go to church on a Sunday, you listen to a lot of stuff about what you ought to do, how you ought to live your life...

You agree.
Yes, you agree. That's why you've gone to church.

But you don't act on the principles you've expressed your support for.
No, you wouldn't need to go to church if you lived like that anyway. You'd be out there doing it.

So what is Australia's position on human rights? We support the UN charter on human rights?
We support the UN charter on human rights, but we are opposed to the UN charter on human rights.

Hang on, Mr Howard. You can't say that. It doesn't make sense.
Doesn't it? Are you sure?

You just said, 'We support the UN charter on human rights, but we're opposed to the UN charter on human rights.'
I see. I can't be on both sides.

That's right. It doesn't make sense. Do you want to answer the question again?
Yes. Ask me again.

Mr Howard, do we support the UN charter on human rights?
In theory, yes.

But not in practice.
We support it in practice in Timor.

But not south of Timor.
No.

We support it in the Gulf.
But not in the Gulf of Carpentaria.

Do we support it in the Falklands?
Yes, but not in the other rural electorates.

The Hon. Michael Wooldridge
Minister for Health

I know who women are. I'm a doctor.

Dr Wooldridge, thanks for your time.
Nice to see you. Sit down. What seems to be the trouble?

You've created a bit of a furore with your remarks about tampons, which attract the GST because they are, of course, a luxury item.
Yes, well, I've apologised for my remarks.

Why did you apologise?
I got told to. John Howard rang and told me to apologise.

Why did he say you had to apologise?
Apparently I'd upset a whole lot of people.

Who were they?
I don't know. Some minority interest group somewhere.

Women?
That's it. That was them, yes. I don't know who's organising them.

You don't know who women are?
Yes. I know who women are. I'm a doctor.

You're trained to tell the difference.
Oh, yes. It's one of the first things you learn.

But you didn't recognise them as a political grouping?
I didn't realise they were working together, no.

I don't think they were, were they? Until you united them.
I've provided them with a point on which they all agree?

Yes.
That's certainly the thrust of a lot of the emails we've been getting.

That you're a little p...?
Yes. That I'm just a little patronising.

Have you done it before?
The tampon routine, 'I beg your pardon, I didn't know menstruation was a disease.'

Yes. The comparison with shaving cream.
Oh, I've done it plenty of times. I'm a doctor. It normally works pretty well.

It's pretty funny, isn't it?
I think it's funny, yes, and as I say it normally goes gangbusters.

Who is your normal audience?
I'm a doctor.

So mostly blokes.
Yes. And a lot of women who want to marry doctors.

They'd find it funny.
Oh. They are the greatest audience.

They'd pick up everything I suppose would they, the women?
Not if they look after themselves they won't.

How are they going to look after themselves?
Yes, we're getting a lot of emails about that.

The Hon. John Howard
Prime Minister of Australia

They were all facing the wrong way.

Mr Howard, thanks for your time.
Well, very nice to be with you. Thank you.

I wonder if I could ask you about the huge turnout for Corroboree 2000?
Yes, certainly. What was the name of the team again?

Corroboree 2000. You know, the reconciliation movement, the walk across the bridge?
Ah, yes. I recall something of the type.

Did the enormous response surprise you?
No, not really. I'm speaking from memory...I think I spoke at it, didn't I?

Yes, you did. You had the opportunity to apologise, too, didn't you?
This was the thing where a whole lot of people were given the wrong map.

A faulty map?
Yes, they were obviously under the impression I was going to be giving a speech from the rear of the hall. They were all facing the wrong way. Every time I looked up...

They had their backs to you?
All I could see were the backs of people's heads and lots of hats.

Maybe the acoustics were bad?
Frankly, I didn't like the look of any of them.

Mr Howard, did you see the speech as an opportunity to offer an apology?

I saw the speech as an opportunity to express some concerns I think a lot of people have about apologising for something that they didn't do.

But the apology that's required isn't about your personal responsibility for what happened.

That's good, because I haven't done anything wrong.

Isn't what's required, Mr Howard, an acknowledgment that what happened did happen?

Well, look, if something happened, obviously somebody did it. And it wasn't me!

You don't have to be the one who did something to feel sorrow for the people it happened to.

Good, OK. Can we talk about something else now? Much though I have enjoyed the thrust of your early questions.

Mr Howard, you recently went to the battlefields of France?

I did, yes. I visited a number of Australian graves and…

You said you were sorry that they'd lost their lives.

It was a tragic loss of life. Absolutely tragic.

Did you kill them?

I beg your pardon?

Did you kill them?

No, of course I didn't kill them. What do you mean, 'Did I kill them?'

How can you be sorry for something you didn't do?

Oh, this is completely different.

Why is it different, Mr Howard?

Well, you yourself said this was in France. It's not even in Australia. It's a completely different country. It's off the coast somewhere.

Do you think anyone actually agrees with you on this issue?
There were a lot of people on the Sydney Harbour Bridge.
Plenty of people agree with me.

Who?
Well, look, my wife's brother works with a woman whose husband is a mechanic at a hospital. The person who runs the hospital, his sister knows a bloke who agrees with every aspect of what I say about this really rather complex question.

Can we ring him?
Certainly, we can ring him. I was talking to him earlier.

And he agrees...
He agrees absolutely with everything I say.

OK, it's ringing.
(Howard's phone rings.) Excuse me for a moment. Hello?

Hello. Mr Howard.
Yes, can I ring you back, mate? I'm just doing an interview. *(He hangs up.)*

Who was that?
I don't know, but don't worry about him.

Why not?
The GST'll get him.

An Employee of the Airline Industry

You can't use them at any time you wish to travel.

Thanks for your time. *(Louder.)* Thanks for your time.
I beg your pardon, you'll have to speak up. I work in the airline industry.

You are with the airlines.
Yes, I know. Have been for many years.

Which one are you with?
I'm with one of the big two. Everyone's with one of the big two. Everyone in the country. There's nowhere else to go. You've got to be with one of them.

Well, which one are you with?
Have you got one in mind?

Yes.
I'm with the other one. I joined them upon leaving school and I've gone rather well since.

It's a very competitive industry, isn't it?
The airline industry in Australia is very, very competitive indeed. We no longer have the two-airline policy.

What was the two-airline policy?
That was an arrangement whereby, if you missed one plane, you could be happy in the knowledge that had you got there a few minutes earlier you would have missed the other one.

Oh, yes. They still have that.
They've still got that?

Yes.
It's a very, very competitive industry.

Does your airline have frequent flyer points?
You'll have to speak up, I'm afraid. I work in the airline industry.

Does your airline have frequent flyer points?
Lashings of them. It's a major incentive scheme of ours, yes.

But you're in a bit of trouble, aren't you, about the conditions under which you can use them?
We are at the moment, yes, but that'll blow over.

According to the rules, when can't you use frequent flyer points?
You can't use them at any time you wish to travel.

Any time you'd want to go anywhere.
That's right.

If there were, say, a special event.
Christmas?

Yes, Christmas, New Year, Easter.
You couldn't use your frequent flyers then, no. They're all excellent examples...

You can't use them when anything's happening.
That's right.

A footy final, Mardi Gras.
Anything of that kind. All 'no go' areas.

So when can you travel?
You can travel at any time when you don't want to go anywhere under any circumstances.

When you've got no reason to travel?
When you can't even think of anywhere you would be interested in going.

When it makes absolutely no sense at all to go anywhere?
The more pointless, the better it fits the regulations, yes.

So what is this scheme?

I'm sorry? I can hardly hear you. I work in the airline industry.

What exactly is this scheme?

It's an arrangement whereby we get rid of a whole lot of seats we can't sell.

No, I mean what is it called? Its technical name?

In marketing terms, it's an incentive arrangement for our very valued customers.

***(Ding Dong!)* Whoops, there's my flight.**

No, son, I think you'll find that's mine. *(Ding Dong!)*

Are you sure?

You'll have to speak up, I work in the airline industry.

The Hon. Kim Beazley
Leader of the Opposition

This is the thrill of a lifetime.

Mr Beazley, thanks for your time.
Rollback. Rollback. Rollback. Rollback. Pardon?

Mr Beazley, thank you for your time.
Rollback.

No. You say, 'It's a pleasure.'
Oh, I beg your pardon. 'It's a pleasure.'

Mr Beazley, thanks for your time.
Hello there. Nice to talk to you.

First of all, Kim, congratulations.
Thank you, very, very much indeed.

You must be pretty excited, aren't you?
I am excited. I'm thrilled. This is the thrill of a lifetime.

If anyone had told you last year you'd be up for an award…
I wouldn't have believed them.

You've literally come from nowhere, haven't you?
Yes. I just did bit parts all last year. I couldn't get a decent role last year.

Of course. And then you did *How the West Was Won*.
That is right. Had a lead in that. Had a wonderful time doing that.

That was really the beginning, wasn't it?
I think it probably was.

And then you did that touring one in the bus in the backblocks?
The road movie?

Yes. What was that called again?
Every Which Way but Policy.

With the orangutan?
With the orangutan, with me in the cab, yes.

Tremendous, yes. Where did you get that orangutan from?
He was an office bearer somewhere in the New South Wales right with nothing better to do.

And then you did the one with Pauline Hanson.
In Queensland?

Yes.
Yes, *The Sting*. Pauline and I did *The Sting* in Queensland.

Yes, the Beattie picture. And I understand you're about to go away and do *Revenge of the Killer Tomatoes*?
No, unfortunately, that's fallen through.

I thought you were up for that.
I was up for it, yes, but I didn't get the part.

Really? Is it still happening? Who's doing it?
John Howard's doing it. They're already shooting.

Who's doing the other part? The Won Nay Shon part?
That's all done with computer animation.

John Howard will need to be a bit careful there, won't he?
He will, yes. But he's done it before. He was terrific in *Crouching Hanson, Hidden Thumping*. Have you seen that?

I have. I thought he was very, very special.
He's pretty good, isn't he?

It's a fantastic film.
It's a very authoritative performance, isn't it? And a very different role for him.

He's normally so straight. Has he ever done this sort of action-comedy before?
Well, have you ever seen him walking in sports clothing in a foreign capital?

I meant in a film.
No, fair point. I don't think he has done it in a film before.

And the effects are great, aren't they?
Spectacular effects.

I love the way he seems to go backwards all the time.
Exactly, yes. All these other characters come into shot and go forward and John Howard goes backwards. It's amazing.

It must be awfully hard.
Technically it must be a nightmare. I was talking to the producer the other day. Apparently it's kind of a computer thing.

Right. So, Kim, tell us. What else have you got on the drawing board?
Actually there's something pretty exciting next, I hope.

Great! What is it?
I'm going to do a thing called *Rollback*.

Great title!
It is a great title, isn't it. Fantastic title, *Rollback*.

What's it all about?
I've got no idea.

Really? Why did you decide to do it?
It's a good role. A very strong, important, principled role.

And a good title.
Great title, fantastic title—*Rollback*.

Have you read the script, Kim?
No, the script's not written yet.

So you don't know what it's about?
Well, I imagine it's about rollback.

What does that mean?
I've got no idea.

Do you have a synopsis?
What they told me is it's about a man who says he's going to roll
something back, but nobody's quite sure what that means.

And you're playing the lead, the man, are you?
I'm playing the man, yes. They just told me to lose some weight and see
if I could make some sense.

Best of luck, Kim.
(Sings.) 'Roll 'em in, roll 'em out, roll 'em up, roll 'em back...'

No, no, Kim, that's *Rawhide*.
Oh, I think it could get a lot worse than that, son.

The Hon. John Howard
Prime Minister of Australia

We've pulled the drawbridge up in this country.

Mr Howard, thanks for your time.
Yes, very nice to be with you, thank you.

You must be very pleased with the polls that came out this week.
No. We don't care who they are. They're not coming out here.
We've pulled the drawbridge up in this country. We made this
announcement. We've had it, we've had it with them.

No, no, Mr Howard. The popularity poll. You're miles ahead.
Yes, I'm a little bit disinclined to put too much store by that sort of
thing.

But you're in full election campaign mode now, aren't you?
We are, yes. We've decided when we're going to the people and it will
be a short campaign but a terribly, terribly important one.

I'm sure. What do you think will happen?
It's very hard to say. And I would say to any of our people out there
who may be vacillating, you mustn't take this for granted. I don't want
people to get at all complacent about this. It's not going to be easy. It's
going to be very close.

Close?
We've introduced, let's face it, some of the most radical reforms seen in
the economic sector in this country in many years and I think people
are often alarmed by change and they may opt for something more
conservative.

More conservative than you are?
Yes. That's why we've got an opposition in this country.

Right. *(Bryan notices a mobile phone.)* **What is that?**
That's my phone.

Is it on?
Yes, of course it's on.

Mr Howard, it's customary when you're doing an interview to turn it off.
You will appreciate that, in the current international crisis, George Bush may ring me at any time.

Yes, I appreciate that.
I need the phone with me at all times, so I'll just leave it there if you don't mind.

Can't he leave a message or something?
George Bush and I have a close personal relationship...

Sure, I understand that.
...particularly at this time of international instability. It is vital that I be able to take George Bush's call at any time.

OK, fine. I wonder if I could ask you about the effect of the GST on Australian business at the moment.
Yes—did you just hear a ringing sound? Was that a ringing sound?

No, I don't think so.
You didn't hear a ringing sound?

No.
'Ring ring', for example?

No. Mr Howard, small business has struggled with the GST, hasn't it? And we now have big business in all sorts of trouble—
You must have heard that slight digital buzzing, then?

No. I didn't hear anything.
You don't think someone's trying to ring? I wouldn't want to miss the call.

No, I didn't hear anything. Mr Howard, consumer confidence is down. Coles Myer's retail figures…

That'll be him now. *(He picks up the phone.)* George? Yes, it's John Howard…Is anyone there?

No, there's nobody there.

I just saw this flickering light—I thought it must be a call.

No, that's the battery light.

Oh, the battery, oh.

Mr Howard, what are you doing about the asylum seekers?

I beg your pardon? Would you repeat the question?

What are you doing about the asylum seekers?

That is a very, very good question. Hold my phone for a minute, please.

Sorry?

This is a very, very important issue for this country. Very, very important. Australia has one of the most staggering, almost unique records in humanatropical matters.

Humanitarian.

Pardon?

Humanitarian.

Those too. Indeed. We have a very good record and we won't be held over a barrel just because the…

Refugees are desperate and we're a very large underpopulated country.

That's right. We're not going to be blackmailed in this country.

Now, Mr Howard, what do I do if this rings?

Oh, take a message. It'll only be George. This is a very, very important issue. We took a refugee into this country in 1984. The record will show that. I think we took another one in 1987.

Hang on, Mr Howard, I think it's the president.

(He picks up the phone.) George? Hello? There's nobody there.

Thanks for joining us.

The Hon. Daryl Williams
Attorney-General of Australia

An absolutely beautiful place. It's got walls.

Daryl Williams, thanks for your time.
It's very good to be here, thank you.

Attorney-General, we're having a lot of problems up in Woomera at the moment, aren't we?
We have been experiencing one or two problems in the Woomera area recently, yes. The people being held in detention there are engaging in what I would describe as acts of destruction.

Wanton destruction.
'Acts of wanton destruction', yes.

Why are the people being held there?
These are people who are waiting for their applications for refugee status to be processed.

And why don't they like being in a jail in Woomera?
I've got no idea.

Is it a nice place?
It's a beautiful place, an absolutely beautiful place. It's got walls.

A roof?
Roof, yes.

Fence?
A beautiful fence. It's got one of the best fences I think I've ever seen in my life.

Really? Any trees?
No trees. But a fantastic fence.

Flowers?
Flowers, no. The fence is a ripper, but there aren't any flowers.

Just walls and roof and the fence?
Yes, an absolutely beautiful fence.

Is it near anything?
The building?

Yes.
Yes. It's very near the fence.

I mean, are there towns nearby?
No, this is a detention centre. It's not a hotel we're talking about.

Is there a visiting area?
What's a visiting area?

You know, a place for people to visit people.
No, nobody's going to be visiting these people. It's in Woomera.

And what do these people want?
They want to have their applications processed and get out.

And become part of the community?
That's right. But they're not going to do that so long as they behave in the way in which they have been. They set fire to the place. We're not going to be intimida—

What would happen if they stop causing problems at the detention centre?
What they've got to understand is that they must stop these acts of wanton destruction. They've got to cease being vandals and settle down.

And what will happen if they do?
If they do, we can then look at the possibility of perhaps engaging in some discussion that might ultimately move towards an application review of some kind, at some stage, in respect of some of these people. And actual processing may result in some instances.

But Minister, isn't that the problem? Isn't that the reason for their actions? That we're not processing their applications?
We're not going to process anything at all under any circumstances, if they keep behaving in the way in which they have been.

Aren't they behaving like that purely because you're not doing these applications for them?
We will refuse to process anything so long as people are acting like this. That's what they've got to understand and that's what I'm indicating to you.

OK. And what happens if they do stop?
If they don't stop, we're not going to process anything. That's the position.

And if they do stop?
Unless they stop, nothing will happen.

So we'll hear their applications if they do stop?
We won't be hearing anything unless they stop. That's what I'm saying to you.

Yes, but if they stop, will we process their applications for them?
Let me put this another way. The way to get us to hear their applications is to stop doing what they've been doing. They've got to stop behaving like vandals.

They've got to stop engaging in acts of wanton destruction?
Wanton destruction, yes. Your term. They've got to stop doing that.

But if they stop the acts of wanton destruction, will we process their applications?
Not if they keep behaving the way they have been.

Daryl Williams, thank you very much.
Thank you. I just wanted to clarify the government's position.

The Hon. John Howard
Prime Minister of Australia

The Monday story? The Tuesday story? Today's story?

Mr Howard, thanks for your time.
It's very good to be with you. Thank you for inviting me in.

I wonder if I could ask you about the babies overboard business?
Yes. Certainly. The story that's coming out now or the story we told at the time?

The story that we're getting now.
This week's story?

Yes.
The Monday story? The Tuesday story? Or the one that's broken subsequently?

Well, perhaps today's story.
Today's story?

Yes.
This morning's story or the one we're using now?

What's the difference?
The point I'm making is I have no intention of discussing the period when Peter Reith was saying one thing and I was saying another.

Neither do I. That's fine.
Look, please don't interrupt. I'm trying to answer your question with honesty and integrity...

Both of them?
Simultaneously, yes. And you're interrupting. That's not very helpful.

OK, I'm sorry.
Neither have I any intention of discussing the period when Peter remembered that he was told it wasn't true but he'd forgotten to tell me.

Why would he have neglected to do that?
Don't interrupt, please. It's not helpful at all.

OK, I'm sorry. Go ahead.
Then of course we had the period when Peter thought he may have told me that the thing was completely untrue but he didn't tell me in English.

Oh, that's right. I remember that. Yes, yes, yes. How long did that version last?
It didn't last very long.

It was almost subliminal, wasn't it?
I don't think that was one of our better ones. Then we stumbled on what I believe is an absolute cracker, which was that we were all grossly misinformed by an incompetent public servant.

Public servant. That's the current version, isn't it?
What's the time?

Seven fifty-five.
Yes, that's still current, I don't think we've found any involvement that Peter Hollingworth may have with this issue as yet.

So what does he do now, Peter Reith?
Since he retired from parliament? Peter was lucky enough to secure employment negotiating government defence contracts. *(Laughs.)*

(Laughs.) Really?
Yes. *(Laughs.)* I'm sorry. I'll try that again, sorry. Just ask me that again.

So what does he do now, Peter Reith?
Since he retired from parliament, Peter has been lucky enough to get a job negotiating government defence contracts. *(Both parties doubled-over laughing, desperately trying to compose themselves.)*

Sorry, that is very funny.
I'm sorry. I apologise.

Can I do it again? So what does Peter Reith do now?
Since he retired from politics, Peter...*(Fighting back laughter.)*...I'm sorry. It took us four hours to get this right in the cabinet room before we could even...

OK. You look that way and I'll look this way. *(They face different directions.)*
Yes. Now ask me again.

So what does Peter Reith do now?
Peter Reith, at the moment, is...*(Explodes with laughter.)*

Maybe we'll move on. Let me ask you another question. Why do you think people would throw their own children into the sea?
Why would anyone believe that parents would throw their children in the sea? That's too hard. Ask me the Peter Reith one again.

OK, all right. So, Prime Minister, what does Peter Reith do now?
Peter Reith has got a job selling government defence contracts. *(Both parties erupt into laughter.)*

A Senior Banking Executive

Just take a number, son.

Thanks for your time.
Take a number, will you? I'll be with you in a minute.

You're one of Australia's leading bankers.
Yes. Just take a number, son. I'll be with you as soon as I possibly can.

How many banks do we have in Australia?
There are three or four of us operating in what is technically described as the banking sector. We're all in—what's that thing called?

Sydney.
No, no. It's in the paper all the time.

Russell Crowe?
No. It's where there are only a few of you and you're pretending there are quite a lot of you and you actually control everything.

Competition?
Competition! We're all in competition with one another.

So why have you closed my branch?
Is this an inquiry?

Yes.
Inquiries down the end there, son.

Well, is there anyone else I can speak to?
Someone else in the bank?

Yes.
No.

Why not?
He's at lunch. Do take a number. I'll get to you as soon as I finish doing this.

But hang on, who am I supposed to talk to?
Is this an inquiry?

Yes.
Inquiries down the end there, son.

It would be a lot easier, actually, if you could just answer my question.
Are you on the internet?

No, I'm not.
What you do is you go on the internet and you go to our website...

But I'm not on the internet.
You've got to be on the internet to go to our website.

But I don't want to go to your website.
You can't do your internet banking without going on the internet. You need to go to our website.

Look, excuse me, I don't want to do my banking on the internet.
I want to go and do my banking at a branch.
Just take a number, son, and go down there. I'll be with you as soon as I possibly can.

There's no one down there.
No one down at inquiries?

No.
But there will be when you go down there.

No, I mean there's no one working down there.
That's right. We're a bank, son. We're not here to provide light entertainment. How are we going to make a quid out of answering a lot of silly questions?

Listen, I can't do my banking because you shut my branch, and I want to know why.
You want to know why we shut your branch?

Yes.
That's an inquiry. Take it down to inquiries.

Where am I supposed to do my banking?
Are you on the internet?

Is this an inquiry?
Of course it's an inquiry. I'm trying to find out if…

Inquiries down the end there.
There's no one there. I'm trying to help you, son. You want to know how to do your banking?

Is this an inquiry?
Of course it's a bloody inquiry.

Inquiries down the end there.
I give up.

Yes, I worked that out. My question is where do I do my banking?
I'm sorry, I'm afraid all our usual methods of avoiding the issue are currently engaged. Your call has been placed in the toilet.

The Hon. John Howard
Prime Minister of Australia

I yelled out that there was a wolf coming.

Mr Howard, thanks for your time.
Pleasure.

This last year has brought about a huge change in the way Australians regard regional security, hasn't it?
It has. There's been a loss of innocence.

Yes, when did this happen? Could you date this for us?
I think it began just before the last election.

Going back, take us over what you've said.
I've tried to best represent the interests and concerns of the Australian public.

But take us back to when all this started. Australians were all living happily here…
Yes.

Minding their own business…
Yes.

And so what did you do?
I yelled out that there was a wolf coming.

Was there a wolf there at that time?
No, but Peter Reith informed me there was a wolf.

Where was he saying the wolf was?
He said the wolf was in the water.

A wolf in the water? What would a wolf be doing in the water? Wolves aren't found in the water, are they?
These wolves were.

According to Peter Reith.
That's right.

And then it turned out they weren't there at all?
As it turned out, yes.

What happened next?
George Bush announced he was going to conduct a war on Iraq.

What did you do when that happened?
I did what I was told.

Yes, but what did you actually say?
I said I'd seen a wolf.

Did you yell this out?
Well, I went on television and said that I'd seen a wolf.

Another wolf?
Yes.

This time in Iraq?
Yes.

You'd seen a wolf in Iraq. And how would you have seen a wolf in Iraq?
I didn't actually see it. George saw it.

And how did you know George had seen a wolf?
He rang me up and shouted 'wolf' down the phone.

'Wolf in Iraq'?
Yes.

So now you'd said you'd seen two wolves.
The one in the water and the one in Iraq, yes.

And how many had you actually seen?
Strictly speaking?

Yes.
I hadn't seen any.

And then what happened?
Then we got attacked by a wolf.

This was in Bali?
Yes, that's right.

And did you see that coming?
No. We had no warning of any kind.

And what were you doing at the time?
I was very busy at the time.

Doing what?
I was on television trying to describe the wolf I'd seen in Iraq.

The wolf you hadn't seen in Iraq.
Yes, well, both of them really.

Which both of them?
The wolf I hadn't seen in Iraq and the wolf I hadn't seen in the water.

So whose fault is all this, do you think?
The wolf's. Let's be quite clear about that.

Of course, Mr Howard.
It was all the wolf's fault. *Look out!*

The Hon. Kim Beazley
Backbencher

I have it in me to be beaten a third time.

Mr Beazley, thanks for your time.
Well, thank you. It's very nice to be here and thank you for the invitation.

Yes, nice to see you again.
We have met before, haven't we? You're, um…

Bryan Dawe.
You're Bryan.

That's right. I interviewed you the first time you got beaten by John Howard.
I remember.

And then I interviewed you the second time you got beaten by John Howard.
Ah, yes. I did recognise you. I just couldn't put a name to it.

Now, I've read this piece in the *Bulletin* and you obviously think that if you can regain the leadership of the opposition you can get beaten again.
I think I have it in me to be beaten a third time. I've had a bit of time to think about this on the backbench.

You have.
I'm not exactly putting my hand up.

You're not exactly holding it down either.
Well, it's all speculative.

You're taking a bit of criticism, though, aren't you?
To a degree. I mean, one or two people have, yes, cleared their throats on the matter.

Because it is Simon Crean's turn to get thrashed.
Technically it's Simon's turn to be beaten by John Howard, yes.

He does have a point.
He does have a point, I agree.

I mean, his point is that he's never been beaten by John Howard and so why should he let you get murdered a third time?
Because I'm so bloody good at it. I've been beaten handsomely twice by John Howard. As you yourself have just said, Simon's never been beaten by John Howard.

Crean's argument is that he's not going so badly. His popularity is at minus twenty-seven.
Yes, but that could come up again. At least with me you know you're going to get belted.

But it is his job to be beaten, isn't it, at the moment?
Yes, technically he is in that role.

In fact, you gave him the job. You stood aside at the last election.
I did, but he's such a novice. I've been humiliated by John Howard twice.

I think we accept that you've got a gift for it. But does it really ultimately matter who gets beaten?
I suppose it doesn't matter as long as somebody gets beaten.

From a party point of view?
From a party point of view, I suppose it doesn't much matter, yes.

As long as you don't win?
As long as we keep the party out of office.

So why not leave Crean alone? Let him have a go.
Well, it's just that I miss it so much. Every few years I used to get beaten by John Howard.

Sure, but if you look at it this way, at least you can say you helped, Mr Beazley.
I suppose I cannot unreasonably make that claim, yes.

I mean, you're the one who refused to take a stand on the asylum seekers.
That's very true, that is true.

You trebled the Green vote.
I did an enormous amount for the Greens when I ran the Labor Party.

And he'd have no show of being humiliated the way he is at the moment if it hadn't been for the work you'd put in earlier.
That's very, very nice of you to say that, Bryan.

Well, that's just what I'm thinking, you know.
Well, thank you. Thank you very much.

It's a pleasure.
I feel better just having talked to you about it.

Well, any time.
It's a bit rough out there, but to get someone who understands, it's just great.

That's quite OK, Mr Beazley.

The Hon. Peter Costello
Treasurer of Australia

Johnny wouldn't give me a go on the bike.

Sit down, Peter.
(Peter sits down.)

What's the matter?
Nothing.

Can I ask you a few questions?
All right.

You don't seem very happy.
I'm all right.

What happened?
Nothing.

Come on, I heard all about it. What happened?
Johnny wouldn't give me a go on the bike. He'll never give me a go on the bike now.

Did he say he would give you a go?
Yes, but he won't. He'll be on it forever. He'll never get off it now.

Hang on. What did he actually say?
He said he'd give me a go.

Didn't he say he'd think about giving you a go?
Yes, but he won't. I'll never get a go on the bike now.

Look, I'm sure he'll give you a go.
When?

When he's ready.
I want a go now. He said I could have a go now.

Johnny's having a go now, and he's pretty good at it. I've seen him going past my office a few times.
You should see him when he's not going past your office. He doesn't even tell the truth. He tells big whoppers about what's going on.

Johnny doesn't tell the truth? What are these big whoppers he's been telling?
If I tell you what the big whoppers are, he'll *never* let me have a go on the bike.

But if you don't tell us what the big whoppers are, you'll be helping him tell the big whoppers.
Yes I know. Bloody Johnny.

He's snookered you a bit here, hasn't he?
I hate Johnny.

Come on, you don't hate him. You're just a bit angry.
I'm bloody furious.

We all get angry from time to time. Look on the plus side. Johnny lets you play with the accounts, and there are people who say you're really not very good at that.
I only got one thing wrong.

Yes, but it was rather a big thing, wasn't it?
No, I only put the wrong price in for Telstra.

But you could have got the right price, couldn't you?
How?

It was in the paper, wasn't it, Peter?
I didn't have a paper.

So what did you do?
I made a price up.

So it looked as if there was a surplus?
Johnny told me to do that. That was Johnny's idea to have a surplus. Bloody Johnny, I hate Johnny.

Look, let John have his turn and then when he's finished, you'll get to have a go. And I'm sure you'll be very good at it too.
I should have had a go a long time ago.

You'll have a go.
Thanks for coming to see me.

That's all right. Feel a bit better now?
Not really.

The Hon. John Howard
Prime Minister of Australia

The acting prime minister would do the job.

Mr Howard, thanks for your time.
Good to see you, Bryan. Very good to be on the program.

I wanted to ask you a few things very quickly.
By all means. Certainly.

Obviously you're not going to be available next week.
Pardon? Why wouldn't I be available next week, Bryan? I think I should be available next week.

Well, not unless they get the dispute sorted out. So, I just want to get a couple of very quick responses from you…
What dispute is this, Bryan?

I'll just throw a couple of questions and if you could just give me some quick responses.
I don't understand. What's the dispute that will keep me unavailable next week?

You've got the actors' dispute looming, Mr Howard, so I will just chuck you a few questions…
Actors' dispute? I don't understand quite how an actors' dispute would make me unavailable next week. What's the…

Well, if you don't sort it out, you're going to be on strike next week.
But how will an actors' strike affect me, Bryan? I'm not an actor.

Mr Howard, of course you're an actor. I've seen you on television.
Of course I'm on television, Bryan. I'm the prime minister of the country.

Yes, and I think you're really good. I think you are the best thing in the series, to be perfectly honest.
I don't know what you're talking about, Bryan. I have absolutely no idea what you're talking about.

Oh, Mr Howard, come on. OK, Mr Howard, if you're not in the country, who takes your job?
The acting prime minister would do the job.

The acting prime minister. Exactly. There you go.
Bryan. I am not...

Hang on. Are you a member of Actors' Equity?
Of course not. Why would I be a member of Actors' Equity?

They'll be after you. They don't like that; working without being paid up.
Why would I be a member of Actors' Equity, Bryan? I'm not an actor.

You're not an actor? But your stand-in is? If you're unavailable your understudy acts in your position? Come on, please, Mr Howard...
I'm not an actor, I assure you.

That's fine. You take that view if you wish. It doesn't matter what you call yourself.
It does matter what I call myself, Bryan—I am called the prime minister! I call myself that and so does everyone else.

And, as I said, you're very, very good. I see you on television every week. You're terrific.
Of course I'm on television! Bryan, I'm on television every week in connection with my work.

Mr Howard, actors are on television in connection with their work all the time. All the time, all of them. Don't be silly.
Bryan, what have you ever seen me in?

I saw you in *WMDs*. I thought you were fantastic. I thought the script was awful, but you were terrific.
I didn't write that script, actually.

I know, and didn't it show. But you were really, really good. I saw you in *The Defence of David Hicks*.
I didn't write that script either, I might say.

No, again, the script was awful, but you were really fantastic. How do you remember your lines?
It wasn't easy in that case. Did you see *Peter Gives up Altogether and Buggers Off?*

I did. Loved it to bits.
Because I did write that.

Did you write that?
Yes.

I thought you were both fabulous in that.
What were your other questions, Bryan, just quickly?

You know what they are. You probably got the script before I did.
OK, we'll cut there thank you. Can somebody ring George Bush? There are holes in this *Roadkill for Peace* script you could drive a truck through.

Hang on, Mr Howard. Isn't it *Roadmap for Peace?*
Oh dear. We've got two problems…get him fast, will you?

Thanks for your time.
That'll be the dinner break, Bryan. They'll need to shift the lights.

The Hon. Alexander Downer
Minister for Foreign Affairs

It's a lovely spot, the Caribbean.

Alexander Downer, thanks for your time.
It's a great pleasure, Bryan, and good evening.

Can you explain the position of David Hicks to us, please?
Yes, indeed. The David Hicks case is one I'm very familiar with.

He's an Australian citizen arrested by the Americans in Afghanistan.
He is, yes.

And what has he been charged with?
He hasn't been charged with anything yet, Bryan. But I'd say he's obviously guilty.

Guilty of what, Mr Downer?
Yes, good point. He hasn't been charged so he can't be guilty of...

How long has he been in jail, Mr Downer?
He's been incarcerated for, I think, about nineteen months.

In Cuba?
In the Caribbean, Bryan, yes. Have you ever been up there?

No, I haven't.
It's a lovely spot, the Caribbean. It's an absolute cracker. If you're ever given the opportunity, I'd whistle up there quick smart.

I'll make a note of that. Mr Downer, has David Hicks seen a lawyer?
I doubt that he would have seen a defence lawyer.

But he would have seen a prosecuting lawyer?
He may have seen one or two prosecution lawyers, yes.

A Cuban?
I would think an American in his case.

Mr Downer, is that fair?
From what I understand, Bryan, he's lucky to see any bloody lawyer at all. He was training with al-Qaeda. He was training in the use of weapons with al-Qaeda.

Mr Downer, who told you that?
The Americans, Bryan. I'm not a fool. I've spoken to the prosecutors.

But he hasn't been tried yet, has he? How long is he going to be there? That is my point.
He's obviously guilty, Bryan.

You keep saying this, but guilty of what?
I don't know what he's being charged with, Bryan, but what I'm indicating to you is he probably bloody did it.

(Sighs.) Mr Downer, are you familiar with the trial of Roger Casement?
Roger Casement?

No? Doesn't ring a bell?
It's not an Adelaide name, Bryan, no.

Roger Casement was a citizen of one country, he was kidnapped in that country, taken to another country and then tried for treason in that second country.
He was taken from one country, removed to another country and tried for treason in respect of that second country, which wasn't the country he came from?

Correct. And then executed.
Executed! Good Lord.

Do you see any similarities?
Yes, I do.

Like what?
Guilty as buggery, the pair of them, Bryan.

The Hon. Mark Latham
Leader of the Opposition

A box? What do you need a box for?

Mr Latham, thanks for your time.
It's very good to be here, Bryan. Thanks for the invitation.

Congratulations, by the way.
Thank you, thank you. It's a great honour for me personally, and a healing time for the party. We move now into the future; into a broad, sunlit upland. *(Bryan is donning protective clothing.)* What are you doing, Bryan?

I'm just getting ready.
Getting ready for what? I don't understand.

I'm going to interview you.
I realise you're going to interview me, Bryan. But what is all this stuff? I'm not fully aware of what you're doing there.

This is a protective helmet and some slightly more resilient, industrial clothing.
To protect you against what?

I've got a couple of questions I want to ask you about the government.
But I don't understand. What's this thing here?

This is just a large bit of plastic. It covers up my suit.
Covers your suit? What are you trying to protect yourself from?

In case I ask you a couple of questions about the US.
You haven't asked any questions at all yet, Bryan.

No, I'm not quite ready. I just want to make sure I'm fully kitted up—
I don't know where the interview is going.

I'm nearly ready.
I think you can over-prepare.

I just want to make certain we're ready, that's all.
A box? What do you need a box for?

I'm going to ask you some questions, maybe, that involve the PM. And the last time I did that...
What happened?

It took a week and a half to clean out the studio.
Well, look, Bryan. If I could say to you and to the broader Australian public, you're not going to need that. That's just silly.

So you've reformed?
I have reformed. I am a completely different person now, Bryan. I've stopped that altogether.

So who are you now?
I'm still Mark Latham, Bryan, but I have a completely different set of personal standards as regards my behaviour.

(Bryan pulls on protective welding goggles.) I won't be long.
You'll be perfectly safe, don't have any anxiety about—

OK. Are you ready?
For the interview? I've been ready for the interview for some time. *(Bryan hides behind his chair, peeping out.)* Where are you going?

Just here.
We're about to do the interview?

Certainly. Are you right?
Yes, indeed.

Mr Latham, what do you think of John Howard aligning Australia with the US?
(The building explodes and a firestorm consumes the area.)

Messrs Mick Keelty, Robert Hill and Mark Latham

I may have misled people the other day.

OK. Now, I'll get to all of you as fast as possible. First, Mick Keelty, thanks for your time.
Pleasure.

You've got a clarification you'd like to make?
Yes, look, thanks for giving me the opportunity. I may have misled people the other day with this statement I made.

This is the one about national security?
Yes.

In your capacity as commissioner of the Federal Police?
That's right.

And what was the difficulty?
Just that the prime minister and I had a different way of expressing things maybe.

Different word use.
No, I don't think either of us used the word 'different'.

What was it that you had said?
I advanced the view that the likelihood of Australia being a terrorist target had increased by our involvement in the War on Iraq.

Yes. And what would you like to say now?
I'd like to say that the likelihood of Australia being a terrorist target had increased by our involvement in the Mittagong Begonia Festival.

The Mittagong Begonia Festival?
Yes, I think that's what it says.

Who is Arthur Sinodinos?
He's the prime minister's begonia bloke.

A begonia expert?
Yes.

How would that cause an increased risk to national security?
You can't be too careful, Bryan.

I'll be all right. I've got a fridge magnet. Robert Hill, you've got a correction to make as well, haven't you?
Yes thanks, Bryan.

You're the minister for defence.
Yes, that's right. Australian federal minister for defence.

And what is your correction?
I said during the week that there are no weapons of mass destruction in Iraq.

And what did you mean?
I meant that there were no weapons of mass destruction in 'Irene Goodnight'.

In 'Irene Goodnight'. In the song 'Irene Goodnight'.
Yes.

No weapons of mass destruction in the song?
None at all.

Well, you should know, you're the minister for defence. Mr Latham, you've got something you wish to correct?
Yes. Gidday, Bryan.

What is it you wish to correct?
I made a statement in the parliament the other day.

Oh yes. What statement was this?
It was about Alexander Downer.

OK, what did you say about Alexander Downer?

I called him a rotten, lousy rotten disgrace.

And you've had time to think about that now, have you?

Yes, I deeply regret that statement. That was inappropriate.

And what do you want to say now?

Alexander Downer is a snobby dickhead from Adelaide.

A different sort of disgrace?

Yes. I shouldn't have said it. I'm sorry, Alexander.

The Hon. Peter Costello
Treasurer of Australia

You've got a family, haven't you?

Mr Costello, thanks for your time.
That's a great family, Bryan, and thanks for the invitation. Good to have a bit of a family with you.

Pardon?
It's good to see you, Bryan. Good to be here.

Mr Costello, this is your ninth budget.
Yes, it's a family budget.

You've got a big surplus.
Yes, the important family was working out what to do with it.

That was the important question.
Family is always an important question, Bryan.

I'm interested in a couple of things you've done here with the surplus.
You've got a family, haven't you?

Have I got a family?
Yes.

Yes.
Yes, have they got families?

Has my family got families?
Yes, your family must have a family or they wouldn't be a family.

I suppose my family has a family, yes.
Very important, Bryan. There's nothing more important in Australia, in our way of life than voting.

Than family.
There's nothing more family in our way of voting, than Australia.

Mr Costello, are you trying to become the prime minister, or the editor of *Good Weekend*?
No, I'm the treasurer, Bryan. I'm very happy being the treasurer.

Every now and again we get these same stories about Mr Howard standing aside for you to take over the leadership of the party.
Yes. Don't know where they come from, Bryan.

They're an accident.
Nobody could have been more surprised than I was to see all this come up again just when I was about to announce a huge surplus.

Are they different stories or the same one just run again and again?
From my reading it looked like the same story but with different photos.

You go out and shoot different photos?
Yes, we did.

Why?
I've got no idea, Bryan.

You don't know how it happens?
No idea.

You're very happy being the treasurer?
I'm delirious. I'm so happy I could do it forever.

Mr Costello, if you were going to qualify for the $3000 for having a baby, and your doctor induced the birth a couple of days before the July 1 qualifying date, could you sue your doctor?
Not if the doctor had a family, Bryan.

So how does this all work, do you get the $3000 in the hospital?
No, you go out of the hospital, take your baby to any post office. It's franked, the parents are given some money to take to the casino and the infant is returned.

Isn't this going to take a lot of women out of the workforce?
Only if women are the ones having the babies.

Mr Costello, thanks for your time.
That's a great family, Bryan.

A Quiz Show Contestant

Is that George on the phone?

**Your special subject is John Howard. Your time starts now.
What will John Howard never bring in? Ever.**
A GST.

Correct. When did John Howard bring in a GST?
The first of July 2000.

Correct. What are weapons of mass destruction?
Sorry. Is that George on the phone?

**Correct. If you know people want a republic, how do you get them to
vote against it?**
You ask them to vote for a republic where they don't get to vote for the
president.

Correct. What is the Kyoto Agreement?
Something to do with coal prices?

Correct. What is the environment?
Pass.

**Correct. What were being thrown overboard into the sea just before
the last election?**
Nothing.

**I beg your pardon. I misread the question. What did John Howard *say*
were being thrown overboard into the sea just before the last election?**
The children of asylum seekers.

Correct. What did he do to prove it?
He released a film of it not happening.

Correct. Who told him the children *were* being thrown in the sea?
The minister for defence said he'd been told by the navy.

Correct. And what did the minister for defence do when the navy denied that?
He resigned and got a job selling defence contracts to the Australian government.

And was there a conflict there?
No. It was Peter Reith.

Correct. What about some of the other people in the Howard ministry. When they've retired, where have they retired to?
To jobs with companies who operate in the fields where they used to be the minister.

Correct. And would this have been worked out beforehand?
Shut your face.

Correct. What does the word 'integrity' mean?
Can you repeat the question?

Correct. If you make a promise and don't keep it, what was it?
A non-core promise.

Correct. Who can get married in Australia?
Marriage is between a man and a woman.

What if they don't like each other?
It doesn't matter if they hate each other's guts as long as one of them is a man and one of them is a woman.

Correct. Why don't we have to listen to senior members of the defence community criticise the government on defence?
They're too old.

Correct. Why don't we have to listen to ex-public servants criticising the government's use of research information?
They're the scum of the earth, public servants.

Can you be more specific?
Get stuffed.

Correct. And at the end of that round your house is worth three times what you paid for it.

Great.

Congratulations.

Thanks. Three times what I paid for it!

Yes. Low interest rates. You're worth a fortune.

He's great, John Howard, isn't he?

He certainly is.

The Hon. Brendan Nelson
Minister for Education

You're pretending to be objective.

Brendan Nelson, thanks for your time.
Just relax, Bryan. Pace yourself.

You've announced plans to get stuck into the universities.
We've announced plans to reform certain aspects of the tertiary
education sector. You see this is where the ABC gets itself into trouble.
There's no need to ask that question in that form. I don't know why
you do it. It gives you away. You've got an ideological position. You're
pretending to be objective. You're working for the national broadcaster.

Who do you work for?
I'm in a different position. I work for the government.

Mr Nelson, I...
No, let me finish, Bryan. You're a public servant. The ABC is owned
by the government, by the taxpayers. Ordinary people paying their tax,
that's where your bread and butter comes from. Your job, if I might say
so, is not to express your own particular poisonous prejudice. It is to
make the program in the best interests of the whole of Australia, this is
the Australian Broadcasting Corporation.

I understand that.
Well, that's good.

May I continue?
You may, but bear in mind the guidelines I've given you.

Certainly. And I thank you for the tips.
Pleasure.

Dr Nelson, you've announced plans to reform certain aspects of the tertiary education sector.
That's right, Bryan, I have.

How are you going to achieve this?
What does it mean in practical terms?

Yes.
We're going to get stuck into the universities, Bryan.

Yes. Why is that, Dr Nelson?
It's ideological. There are ideas being expressed in the universities at the moment that are not the government's.

Hasn't that always been the case?
It has, Bryan. It's taken us a while to wake up to it but we're on to it now.

Are there other places where there are ideas being expressed which aren't the government's?
Outside the universities is the other main venue for dissent.

You believe that the universities should be controlled by the federal government?
I do. *(He looks to the back of the room.)* Who is that giggling? Come on. Share the joke.

Dr Nelson. You've said you don't think university students should have to join a student union.
That's right. I don't think the Australian public wants its money spent on a lot of radicals running about the country doing as they please. *(He looks to the back of the room.)* Who said that's what taxpayers are doing? Who said this government is a bunch of radicals who aren't acting in the best interests of the country? I can wait. I've got all day. This has happened before, hasn't it?

Not since you were here last.
We'll wait, Bryan.

Are we staying in?
Yes. You can bang the dusters together. Come on. Bang bang.

The Hon. Kim Beazley
Leader of the Opposition

I'm the leader of the opposition.

Thanks very much for your time.
Very good to be here. Good evening.

You are...Mr?
Kim Beazley.

Kim Beazley. That's right. How are you? I haven't seen you for a bit.
No. I'm very well thanks. How are you?

I'm good, thanks. Now you're doing the job of...
I'm the leader of the opposition.

Yes. Mark Latham's old job.
Yes. Mark's no longer with the firm.

Where is Mark now?
Mark's working from home.

Who was in Mark Latham's old job before Mark Latham?
The way we look at it, it's not Mark Latham's old job. It's my job.

Yes, but who was in the job before Mark Latham?
Simon Crean was.

And before that?
I was, before that.

And before that?
Before me?

Yes.
Me again. But look, you seem to be concentrating on the past. We're a party of the future. We have a forward-looking view...aren't you going to interrupt me?

No, I was going to see what you had to say.
I haven't got anything to say. I was just making the point that we're the party of the first part...

...(Helping.) of the future.
Of the future.

My point is that you go back a fair way. You were the last leader but two and the last but three.
That's right.

When were the Crusades?
The Crusades were before that. My position is similar to that of John Howard. He had about six goes at being leader before he won an election.

And why was that?
The Liberal Party was shell-shocked. They'd been humiliated in a few elections on the trot. They didn't know what they were...Didn't know how best to get the man obviously best suited to manage the country, into the driver's seat.

You nearly won the federal election in 1998, didn't you?
I did. I came within a...

A win.
I came within a win of winning that one.

And you came within a win of winning again in 2001.
I did. The only thing that preventing us from winning that one was the...

The fact that you had the same policies as the government?
Not so much that but that they had them first.

So you had some bad ideas?
We had plenty of bad ideas.

But you didn't have them first.

That's right, and that told against us.

Did you toy with the prospect of having any good ideas, at any stage?

Yes, I'm pretty sure we looked at that.

Wouldn't work?

I think someone suggested that. Perhaps some of the women.

You don't think it would work?

It wasn't up to me. I was only the leader of the party.

So who runs the party if not the leader?

I've got that here. *(He takes a card from his pocket and reads.)* A bloke called…Who's this? I didn't know there *was* a Rupert Packer.

That's two cards.

I see. *(Off.)* Harry, what's the name of the bloke who ultimately sets ALP policy at the moment. That's it. John Howard.

Thanks for coming in.

The Hon. Malcolm Turnbull
Parliamentary Secretary to the Prime Minister

Some of these people have never had a proper job.

Mr Turnbull, thanks for your time.
Good evening, Bryan.

You've been in some trouble with your party leadership this week.
Only because they've got no idea what they're doing.

Why don't they know what they're doing?
They're completely out of touch. They've got no idea. Some of these people have never had a proper job.

You've been particularly critical of the government's tax policy.
Yes. Can we swap seats?

No, I think I'll stay here. Mr Turnbull, you've been critical of the government's tax policy.
The whole country is critical of it. Why wouldn't they be? We've got the highest taxes in our history and some of the richest people aren't paying any tax at all. *(He moves closer.)*

What are you doing?
I'm working for tax reform. *(He moves closer.)*

Can you get back over there?
Back where?

Back to where you were.
I thought it would be better if we were together.

I prefer you over there. Mr Turnbull, you're in an odd position here, aren't you?
Yes, I'd rather be over there.

What I mean is, you're part of the government.

That's right.

So what do you say to people who say your primary loyalty is to the party?

My primary loyalty is obviously to the country and if my party is doing something counterproductive and very stupid, like taxing some of them to the point where they can't afford to stay in business and leaving corporate loopholes you could drive a truck through, then I'll say so.

My point is that at the moment you're doing more damage to the government than the opposition is.

I'm opposed to what the government is doing. What do you expect me to do? Sit there and do nothing like Costello and Hill and these other laureates?

My point is...

I reckon you'd be better here.

I'm happy here, thanks.

(To cameraman.) On me a bit more, thanks. If Bryan's saying something interesting by all means cut to him. But if he isn't, keep it on me.

I'm the talent.

Mr Turnbull. The director of the show will decide who the camera should be on.

On me.

Mr Turnbull.

Can I speak to the director of the *(To Bryan.)* what's the show called? *(He dials a phone number.)*

The 7.30 Report.

Director of *The 7.30 Report* please. Yes. I'll wait. On me. I know who I'll ring. *(Kerry O'Brien closes the show. As he does so, his phone starts ringing.)*

The Hon. John Howard and the Hon. Peter Costello

You don't even know how to have a go on the bike.

All right. Sit down, the pair of you. Goodness gracious me. How many times do we have to have this conversation? I've got you both in here together and you are staying in after school until we sort this matter out. Now, Peter, what is going on?
P: Nothing.

Peter, please don't tell me nothing is going on. I saw the two of you speaking to each other the way you did the other day. Now, it's just not good enough. Everyone heard it. John, what is going on?
J: I wasn't here the other day. I was, er, down the shops.

You weren't down the shops, John, you were here—I saw you. Look, the problem we've got here is you are both senior boys. Do you understand the effect this is going to have on some of the young ones if they see what you are doing? Now, Peter, what is going on?
P: Well, John won't let me have a go on the bike. Everyone knows it's my turn next. It's on the noticeboard. It's been on the noticeboard for ages and he goes round and round and round. He's selfish. He's never going to give me a go on the bike. I'm never going to get a go on the bike now.
J: You don't even know how to have a go on the bike. I mean, it's no use you saying you want to go on the bike. You keep saying you want a go on the bike. It's no use if I'm really good at going on the bike and I pull over and give it to you and you go and hit a wall because you don't even know what you're doing on the bike. That's no use at all.
P: You said you would give me a go on the bike.

All right, boys.

J: Well, I will. I just haven't finished yet. I will give you a go.

P: You're never going to finish. You just said you'd give me a go on the bike so I don't push you off.

All right, boys.

J: You couldn't push a pumpkin down a hill, you great puff-ball.

Boys! Boys!

P: You're an idiot.

J: You stink.

P: Your bum sticks out, anyway.

All right. Listen. Enough is enough. I expected a little bit more maturity, particularly from you, John. Please. Are you going to give Peter a go on the bike at some stage?

J: Yes.

Well, when?

J: Later.

P: Yes, what does that mean? I'm never going to get a go on the bike. *(Repeats.)* I'm never going to get a go on the bike!

Listen, stop it. OK. I'll tell you what concerns me about this, both of you. It is this: while you've been arguing, a truck has driven over the oval; there are big skid marks everywhere. On top of that, the goal posts are missing, and the science block has burnt down. Incidentally, do either of you boys know a boy called Downer?

J: No.

P: No.

Well, he's got his head stuck in the toilet. I've rung Mr Kyoto, I've rung Mr Hicks and Mr Corby. I can't get in contact with any of them. And the bank manager, on top of all this, has rung and said we're $5 billion in debt.

J: Well, Peter...

And I don't know what you boys think you are doing, but I'm just about sick of both of you. Get out!

J: Do you want a go on the bike?

P: No, it's your bike.

Go on, clear off! I'm sick of the both of you. Turnbull! Tell Malcolm to get in here, will you. Hurry up!

J: Turnbull?

P: Turnbull?

J: Bloody hell.

The Hon. John Howard
Prime Minister of Australia

I support those Australians who were there at Gallipoli.

Mr Howard, thanks for your time.
Nice to be talking to you.

Yes, there's been some discussion about Anzac Day this year, hasn't there?
Yes, there has, Bryan, and I've made my position as plain as I can get it. I support those Australians who were there at Gallipoli. I don't have a problem with their behaviour. I was proud to be their commanding officer.

Mr Howard, I was actually meaning the meaning of Anzac Day altogether.
I've seen it said that they perhaps got on the turps and left some crap lying about on the peninsula, but they are Australians. I mean, you get with your mates, you have a couple and lose track of what's going on and you make a bit of a bloody mess. We do that at home, Bryan. I don't see the difference.

Mr Howard, I wondered if the meaning of Anzac Day has somehow changed?
Anzac Day is a day of great importance in the Australian calendar, Bryan.

What do you think that importance is?
Well, I think the essential lessons and characters of Anzac Day are as they have always been, Bryan.

And what are they?
Well, it celebrates that very important time when the Australian government made a very significant decision, Bryan to…

To do as it was told by an imperial power.
…to assemble a very, very impressive body of young men, very talented, very resourceful young men and to send them away to…

Invade another country.
…to defend Britain.

By invading Turkey.
And the way they did it, Bryan, was of the utmost importance because for a start they were…

Landed in a wrong place.
…as I say, a very resourceful group of people. When you try to get into the AIF in the very first lot of volunteers, Bryan, you couldn't get in if you were under six foot one so, obviously our…

Graves were a little longer.
…army was a very impressive body of men and they were led by generals who were…

On a boat a couple of miles off the coast.
…dealing with a pretty significant problem. I mean they had a difficult task. That terrain—I've been over the land, Bryan, and it's very difficult land. I've done that, and a lot of the generals at the time…

Hadn't bothered to…
…they weren't given that opportunity because they were obviously…

Tucking into a bit of dinner.
…trying to deal with the bigger picture and there was a bigger picture because Anzac Day doesn't only celebrate Gallipoli. I mean, the First World War, Bryan, is full of other…

Cock-ups.
…very, very famous battles and this is where Australia comes of age. This is where we stand astride centre stage and become a nation. I mean, obviously the empire is not there anymore. We're in charge of

our own destiny now. Now when Australia wants to know what it's doing in the future it certainly doesn't look to Britain. What we do now is…

Ring George.

…hang on, I've got to ring George. I just got a message to ring George.

No, Prime Minister, that was me.

The important thing, Bryan, is that Anzac Day is very, very, very important to all…

Politicians.

Almost sacred, you might say, Bryan, to all…

Advertising sales.

…to all Australians.

Prime Minister, thanks for your time.

Yes, good on you. Now bugger off, I'm going to talk to George, Bryan, about Australia. We'll let you know. *(Into phone.)* George, John Howard. Howard.

The Hon. Philip Ruddock
Attorney-General

We will be giving the authorities certain powers.

Mr Ruddock, thanks for your time.
A very good evening to you, Bryan.

I wonder if I could ask you about this new legislation that's coming in.
Yes, this is the anti-terrorist legislation?

Yes.
Yes, that legislation has been on the books for some time.

These are amendments, aren't they?
We are bringing in some amendments, yes.

And what is the purpose of them?
Well, we will be giving the authorities certain powers, Bryan, the better to defend Australia from terrorism.

What sort of powers, exactly?
They'll be able to enter premises, for example, where they think there might be terrorist activity.

And arrest people?
And arrest people, by all means. We hope they will, yes.

And what will they arrest them for?
Well, they might, for example, think they know something.

They might know what?
Something maybe they shouldn't know, Bryan.

What sort of thing?
That's not specified in the legislation. This would be a matter for them.

So, they could arrest me?
Theoretically, Bryan, yes, if they thought you perhaps knew something.

What sort of thing would I know?
As I say, Bryan, this is not specified in the legislation. This would be a matter for the arresting officer.

But, Mr Ruddock, how would I establish my innocence here?
Well, you wouldn't be innocent, Bryan, if you were being arrested, would you? They are not going to arrest you if you are innocent. They're not fools, these people.

How do I get out of this?
You'd have to establish, in some persuasive way, that perhaps the thing that they thought you knew, you don't know.

How do I do that?
I have no idea, Bryan. That's not my problem.

But I would have to prove that I didn't know it.
That's it. It's fairly simple.

But isn't that the opposite of the presumption of innocence?
Bryan, this is not a normal situation.

In what way isn't it a normal situation, Mr Ruddock?
Someone has come into your house, Bryan, and arrested you because they think you might know something.

Yes, and it's up to me and I have to prove that I don't know it.
That's correct. It's not a normal situation.

Do they tell me what it is that I don't know?
No, they're not going to tell you what it is.

Why not?
Bryan, if I came into your house and arrested you because I thought you might know something, I wouldn't be able to tell you what it is without impeding your capacity to argue that you didn't know what it was.

In that case perhaps no arrest should be made until the alleged offence can be established, Mr Ruddock.
We don't want them to know. We're not going to tell them, Bryan.

But if you don't tell them what it is, how can they possibly argue that they didn't know it? They don't know what it is, Mr Ruddock.
That's right. I think you'll find we've got them there, Bryan. I don't think they've got a leg to stand on, myself, and they deserve everything they've got coming.

When is this legislation coming in?
After 1 July, when we don't have to trouble the scorer much. We'll run both houses.

And you wrote this?
I'm not alone, Bryan. There were several of us there.

Who?
Oh, there was me, Lewis Carroll, a bloke called Escher from South Australia; a few of us.

Do you know what I think of this legislation, Mr Ruddock?
Be a bit careful here, Bryan.

Do you know what I think of this legislation?
Be a bit careful what you say. *(Public announcement.) Bryan Dawe, to the front desk, please. There are some gentlemen here to see you.*
Don't look at me, Bryan. You got yourself into this.

Peter, A Quiz Show Contestant

I wouldn't mind becoming a prime minister.

OK. Our next contestant. Your name is Peter?
Yes, that's right, yes.

What do you do, Peter?
I'm a treasurer.

A treasurer. My, that must be an interesting job, is it?
Yes, it can be a bit repetitive sometimes. I wouldn't mind becoming a prime minister at some point.

Well, good luck, Peter. Your special subject tonight is right-wing incidents in the life of Christ.
That's correct.

Your time starts now. Name one right-wing incident in the life of Christ.
He threw the money lenders out of the temple.

Can you be more specific?
Yes. He went into the temple and there were money lenders there and he became very angry and tipped their tables over and told them they were usurers and threw them out; biffed them out of the place altogether; threw them out of the temple.

What I meant was, how was that a right-wing thing to do?
Yes, I see. It probably isn't, is it?

Can you think of anything else, Peter?
Yes. He fed 4000 people at one time by sharing food.

How much did he charge for that food?
No, he didn't charge for the food, Bryan. He shared his food. They were hungry and he broke up food. It was loaves and fishes. You've probably heard the story.

I know the story. I'm trying to find the right-wing element in feeding people who need food.
Yes, I see. There probably isn't one, is there? He healed the sick.

Yes.
But actually I think he probably did that for nothing. In fact, I think he probably did that because he loved mankind.

It's not really a right-wing mantra, is it?
It's not a *central* tenet of capitalism, the laying on of hands, no.

He made the lame walk, too, didn't he?
He did, and he forgave the people who killed him.

Did he stick any people in detention centres?
Oh, no, I don't think he would have approved of that at all. He got one bloke up from the dead. A bloke was dead and he made him walk.

This is Lazarus?
Lazarus. Yes. He healed him completely. I don't think he would have approved of putting people in a detention centre, no.

Peter, would you like to reconsider your special subject tonight; right-wing incidents in the life of Christ...
No thanks. I'll think of something, Bryan. I'll have to come up with something sooner or later.

Why is that?
Oh, for this other project I'm working on.

You've snookered yourself a bit here, Peter, haven't you?
No, Bryan. I know! He said at one stage it would be as difficult for a rich man to enter the kingdom of heaven as it would be for a camel to pass through the eye of a needle.

Oh, I'll have to check that with the adjudicator, Peter. Hang on. Can we accept that? Yes, sure. Hang on, I'll ask. Peter, what is your net worth?
(Peter is appalled and realises he cannot win.)

A Quiz Show Winner

Sorry, can you repeat the question?

Your special subject is Australian government policy. Your time starts now. Official government policy is to sell Telstra?
Correct.

Or to retain ownership of the half they still own?
Correct.

For two different prices.
Correct.

To the people who already own it.
Correct.

Against the wishes of the Australian public.
Do you mean all of the Australian public?

I mean the great majority. Australia is a democracy.
(Guessing.) Correct.

Did the government put any condition on the sale?
Yes, but they did it anyway.

Correct. What was the condition?
That telephone services be improved in the bush.

Correct. And did they improve the services in the bush?
Sorry, can you repeat the question?

Can you be more specific?
I can hardly hear you.

Correct. What did Telstra used to spend its money on?
On research and development in telephony.

What did it spend its money on in recent years?
On returning a dividend to shareholders.

Correct. Why is Telstra not worth as much money as the government thought it was?
Because it has missed the boat on the new developments in technology and telephony.

Correct. Why?
Because it didn't spend enough money on research and development.

Correct. Why not?
Because it's been spending its money on returning a dividend to shareholders.

Correct. Why can't the government force Telstra to provide a proper service to the Australian public?
Telstra's a public company.

Correct. Why can't Telstra concentrate on the services where the money really is?
Because it's run by the government.

Correct. Who is Telstra's biggest shareholder?
The government.

Correct. Why?
Because they can't afford to sell it.

Correct. Why did they want to sell it in the first place?
Pass.

'To give Australians an opportunity to purchase a stake in this great national institution.'
(Snorts.) That can't be right—it's completely stuffed!

Hang on a sec. *(Seeks an adjudication.)* Tony, can we accept 'stuffed'?
T: Bloody oath we can; we were opposed to it in the first place and now it doesn't work as a service and it's missed the boat as a company.

***(Both.)* Correct!**

Mark Latham
Previous Opposition Leader

I've certainly cut a bit of a swathe.

Mr Latham, thanks for your time.
Nice to be with you, Bryan. How are you?

I'm good, thank you.
Good on you, Bryan.

Gee, you've cut quite a swathe this week.
I don't know about a swathe, Bryan, but I've certainly cut a bit of a swathe during the week.

It's a tough business, isn't it, politics?
I don't know about tough, Bryan, but I'll tell you something about this business, it's pretty tough. Pretty tough.

Didn't you know it was going to be tough when you went into it, though?
Yes, yes. You don't go into a business like this, Bryan, without knowing it's going to be tough. I knew it would be tough. I knew it would be tough. I knew it would be tough.

Did anything surprise you about it, though?
Only the toughness, Bryan. Only the toughness.

But you would have expected that, wouldn't you?
I did. You don't go into a business like this, Bryan, without knowing what to expect.

But were you surprised when it turned out to be so tough?
I wasn't surprised in the sense that it surprised me.

It's just that you didn't expect it?
Exactly. Exactly. Exactly, Bryan. Exactly.

Mr Latham, when did you first realise they were all against you?
When they made me leader of the Labor Party.

And who did that?
They all did. The whole bloody lot of them. They all got together, all of them, literally all of them. And they ganged up on me. They made me the bloody leader of the Labor Party.

And did you expect that?
Well, not to the extent that it happened, Bryan, no.

Did you *want* to be leader of the Labor Party?
Well, I was in the party forever, Bryan. I've been in the party for years and years and years and years and years and years and years and years.

A long time?
So in a way it was kind of an honour to lead these scum.

So you were proud?
I don't know about proud, Bryan, but I tell you something, it makes you proud when it happens. It makes you proud when it happens.

And who was there when they chose you?
Well, there was a bunch of us there. There was me, Dinsdale Piranha and a bloke called Kierkegaard who just sat there biting the heads off whippets.

Kim Beazley?
Beazer was there. Wayne Swan was there. Good to see Barry Hall in the team, isn't it? Good to see Barry got off. Isn't that good news?

Yes. Different sort of Swan, though.
Yes, but it's good to see a bloke getting off a charge of clouting people. I reckon that's quite good.

Oh, you like that?
That's the Australian way for my money, Bryan. That's the Australian way, isn't it?

Mark Latham, thank you very much for your time. Good luck with the book and thanks for coming in.

Yes, well, you can start any time you like now, Bryan.

Pardon?

Ready to roll when you are, Bryan.

We just finished.

Yes, but you don't know what you want to say until it's all over, do you? It doesn't matter until it stops mattering. You don't know what you're going to say until you finish doing the stuff. *(Looks away.)* You see that bloke over there?

Yes.

That's me.

(Concerned for Mr Latham's health, Bryan wraps it up.) **Right. Thanks for your time.**

The Hon. Kevin Andrews
Minister for Workplace Relations

Bryan, can I have a private word with you?

Mr Andrews, thanks for your time.
Good to be with you, Bryan. Good evening.

You've dismissed huge demonstrations this week against your IR legislation.
Yes, they were fairly predictable. We thought that'd probably happen.

Will they have any effect?
No, of course they won't. Ninety-five per cent of people went to work.

So we won't be doing any AIDS research in this country?
No AIDS research? Why not? I don't see...

Well, ninety-five per cent of Australians don't have AIDS.
Bryan, my point is that the unions are an archaic, smokestack organisation. It's not surprising to me that their mode of expression is basically irrelevant.

What should they have done?
A touch of the forelock wouldn't have hurt, I'd have thought.

Mr Andrews, there's a fair old alliance against you in this. It's not just the trade unions, is it?
Bryan, can I have a private word with you? You've got a bit of a problem here. I saw you involved in these protests. You marched in the street the other day...

Like a lot of Australians who have concerns about what you're trying to do here.
Well, you're biased aren't you, Bryan? I'd rather talk to someone who's not biased on this issue.

So would I.
I am not biased. You think I'm biased?

Of course you're biased.
We're not biased. We're the government. We're the government of the country.

Of course you're biased. You're bringing in this legislation.
I wasn't running about in the bloody street the other day, protesting against what's going on in this country.

Yes, which also concerns me. You think this is all right.
Bryan, I know it's all right. We've shown it to the Business Council. They reckon it's an absolute cracker.

Why don't the churches think it's a good idea?
Because they're biased.

Why don't the social welfare bodies think it's a great idea?
Because they're biased. Why do you think employer organisations and the Business Council reckon it's such a pearler?

They're biased.
Oh don't be ridiculous, Bryan, they're the people who understand the economy best.

Mr Andrews, would you agree that the government's IR reforms take power away from the employees and give it to management?
That's a very broad generalisation.

It may well be, but is it true?
As it happens it is true but it's a very broad generalisation and I want you to understand its broadness.

Will there be a Fair Pay Commission for executives?
No, that's not what the Fair Pay Commission is, Bryan, it's not for executives. Why do you ask?

Because if people see executives paying themselves these obscene amounts of money and workers are having their conditions taken away from them...

...they might get biased, yes.

They might get very biased indeed, Mr Andrews.

It's a fair point, Bryan.

Will you do something about that?

We might have to do something about that.

What will you do?

Keep executive packages out of the paper for a fortnight until we've got away with it.

It's a pity Telstra announced they were firing 12,000 people this week, wasn't it?

Yes, the timing wasn't terribly good, Bryan. Of course there's nothing the government can do. The government doesn't own Telstra.

And whose decision was that?

Bryan, I'm happy to talk about IR reform, but I'd rather talk to someone who isn't biased, do you understand that?

Exactly my position. Couldn't agree more. Thanks for joining us.

You're fired.

The Hon. John Howard
Prime Minister of Australia

The national anthem, Bryan. I think we should stand.

Mr Howard, thanks for your time.
Pleasure, Bryan. Good to see you and thanks for inviting me on the program. *(An anthem begins. Mr Howard stands.)*

What's that?
The national anthem, Bryan. I think we should stand.

Why is the national anthem playing?
Because Australia is doing so well. It's a terrifically successful country.

Mr Howard, it's hard to have a serious conversation while all this is going on.
You'll get used to it, Bryan. It's not everyone's cup of tea but it's the way we do things at the moment and it seems to work well.

It's a bit distracting, this, isn't it? How do you concentrate?
I am concentrating.

Don't you find it a distraction?
I find it rather relaxing. People love it.

How are we supposed to have a sensible discussion about anything?
Normal business goes on all the time. I make announcements about government policy all the time.

That's what concerns me. They used to interrupt a cabinet meeting if Australia won the Ashes. Now you don't interrupt sport to have a discussion about government policy.
Yes, we do, Bryan.

No, you don't. You announced your new IR legislation during the Melbourne Cup.
Yes, but we didn't bring it in until the Commonwealth Games.

Were you at the closing ceremony?
Yes, it was magnificent.

What did you especially like about it?
It kept the uranium deal we've done with the Chinese out of the papers.

And you've decided to restructure the board of the ABC?
Yes, we did that during the swimming.

Can I ask you about this cyclone that went through Queensland?
Larry.

Yes, why did it happen?
I don't know. It's weather isn't it, cyclones?

Have we signed the Kyoto Protocol yet?
I don't know. I'd have to check.

Who would you check with? You're the prime minister.
I'd need to check with the minister for selling coal.

Can you just sign this, please?
What is it?

It's an acknowledgment that we had this conversation, that I asked you about environmental damage and cyclones.
Why do you want a signed document?

We don't want the government to say it wasn't told about the connection between global warming and weather change.
Why would the government deny it had been told something?

Do you know anything about how the international wheat trade works?
No, but I could ask Alexander Downer.

Why ask Alexander Downer?
He won't know either. He's very reliable. Wave to that bloke.

Who is he?

John So. He's famous. Hello John.

What are you going to do when this music finishes?

They'll start the Anzac Day music any minute.

The Hon. Kim Beazley
Leader of the Opposition

Would you like to ask me some questions?

Mr Beazley, thanks for your time.
Pleasure. Good to be here.

Yes. *(Bryan relaxes. He smiles at his guests.)*
Would you like to ask me some questions?

No thanks. Just happy to have you here.
Why am I here if you don't want to ask me anything?

We need balance.
Balance?

Yes, balance in the program.
Balance.

The ABC is very concerned with balance.
What is balance?

I've got no idea. It's not a decision I make. It's upstairs.
Balance with what?

We've had the prime minister in a couple of times. We need to balance that out.
With me.

Yes.
How do I balance the prime minister?

You're still with the Labor Party?
Yes, I'm the leader of the Labor Party.

Yes. Even better.
So what do we do?

Doesn't much matter. How's the economy?
Hard to say.

The war in Iraq?
Very difficult to say. Not really our war.

Health? Education? IR? The environment? What are you doing?
I thought I might try to finish the crossword.

That's 'apathy'.
What is?

That one ending with a y.
Which one?

Six-letter word meaning 'laziness or want of energy'.
No, I've got that one.

What is it?
'Policy'.

Policy?
Apathy? Could be. So what's this one down here?

What is it?
He was *blank* to be elected into high office for a decade.

How many letters?
Ten.

Triumphant.
Oh.

What did you have?
Wilderness.

No, it ends in a t.
Why?

Because that one across is Green voters.
'A generation of disaffected young people'?

Yes. What have you got?
Bugger them.

That doesn't fit.
It does if you colour a couple of these other squares in black.

What's that big one running down the side?
'Reason given for the war in Iraq'.

Thanks for coming in.
Doesn't fit.

No, I'm thanking you.
Oh. Have you got a rubber?

A Mining Engineer

There was some life down there.

Thanks for coming in.
Good evening, Bryan.

You must be happy this great drama is over.
Fantastic achievement by everyone involved.

Yes. Can you describe the actual engineering problem?
Yes, the ground level is here and the…

I've seen the diagrams in the paper.
Yes, they show it pretty well.

It is amazing. Take us through it. How did it start?
Originally there was a sort of collapse.

In the ALP?
Yes, in the main shaft.

The polls had given way.
Yes. But we got some thermal-imaging equipment and it showed that there was some life down there.

This is underneath?
Yes, a long way down.

This was Bill Shorten.
Yes, but he was a long way down and he was trapped under a very heavy rock.

But he was OK?
Yes he seemed to be.

What had happened?
A large Beazley had become dislodged and had fallen into the shaft.

Above him.
Yes, and there was no way that was coming out.

It couldn't be winched to the surface?
No, it was wedged.

Too heavy?
And everything underneath it was trapped.

Could you drill through the Beazley?
We could but we had to be very careful.

You didn't want to get into worse trouble.
No, and then the Beazley turned out to be a lot thicker and harder than we thought.

Five times the density of concrete, I was told.
Yes. Belt it with a crowbar it doesn't even leave a mark.

Hence the delay.
Yes, which is why it took us so long.

How was Bill going through all this?
Remarkable. The resilience of the guy.

How did he keep his spirits up?
We were getting messages to him through a tube.

How was he?
He was good. He knows all the words to 'My Way'.

And then he walked out?
He walked out, waving.

Will the mine be closed?
That's a decision that'll be made over ensuing days.

Have the TV networks talked to Bill Shorten? This is an amazing story.
It is. It's astonishing. I imagine Bill is talking to the networks.

What will those discussions be about?
I don't know.

But Bill knows all the words to 'My Way'?
He does, and he'll bring his own lights.

A Voter

A wonderful place to bring up petrol prices.

Thanks for your time.
Thanks for inviting me in.

I wonder if I can just go through some of your responses to these questions.
Yes, which ones?

You're a voter?
Yes.

Where are you?
We're in Mortgage Vistas.

OK.
Up the Gearing Highway.

Whereabouts?
It's about an hour and a bit up there. You know where the Kiddies are?

Yes.
Through there and it's about another 2.5 per cent.

Near Dreamy Peaks.
Yes, you've gone a bit far there. It's between Dreamy Peaks and Bigborrowings.

What's that river up there?
The Barrel.

Yes, that's beautiful.
Gorgeous. Take a camera if you go up there. You look directly down the Barrel from Bigborrowings.

Yes. It's lovely country up there.
It's a wonderful place to bring up petrol prices.

Children.
You're telling me.

OK, and you were polled recently?
No, I think that's just these new trousers.

I mean you've been questioned by pollsters.
Yes, sorry, that's correct.

And you've said you believe Peter Costello's version of the meeting with John Howard.
Yes. *(Off.)* Interest rates haven't gone up have they? Still eight per cent?

But you don't want Peter Costello as prime minister.
That's right. *(Off.)* Let me know if they go up. They're still eight per cent?

And you've put Kim Beazley ahead of John Howard as preferred prime minister.
Yes, that's right.

So if there was an election you'd vote for Kim Beazley.
No we wouldn't. John Howard's the prime minister. *(Off.)* Interest rates? Still eight per cent?

So why have you said you'd vote for Kim Beazley?
John Howard's got to know this IR stuff stinks. We're not having that. That's terrible. That's not the way we treat each other in Australia.

Have you said that anywhere here?
Yes.

Where?
We said if there was an election tomorrow we'd vote for Kim Beazley.

What'll you do if interest rates go to ten per cent?
They're not going to do that are they?

I don't know. Nobody can control interest rates.
Give us a ring if interest rates go to ten per cent.

And what'll you do?
I'll tell you what I really think of John Howard.

The Hon. Kim Beazley
Leader of the Opposition

I've looked at John Howard for a long time.

Mr Beazley, thanks for your time.
Very good to be with you, Bryan.

How are things going?
Very well, thanks.

Are you busy?
I have been busy.

You're on the road a lot, aren't you?
I am. I've been in Sydney, Brisbane, Melbourne, Canberra.

And are you getting a good response?
By and large, yes. There are critics, of course. Not everyone likes it.

They'll always be critics, I suppose.
Exactly. But generally I think things are good.

You're getting good notices in the press.
Yes. You need plenty of coverage. You can build from there.

It's quite an achievement. How do you do it—the John Howard impression? Because you don't look like very like him.
No, but I've lost some weight and the John Howard impression's not the only thing I do.

I know but that's what you're best known for. How do you think your way into the character?
I've looked at John Howard for a long time. I studied the way he talks, the sort of things he says, the way he stands.

What sort of thing does he say?
He has quite conservative views. He's all for big business. He's a nationalist; he's very big on the army.

Yes, you've caught all those things perfectly.
He's very keen on the popular media; he's on talkback all the time.

Just like you. It really is uncanny.
He gets photographed a lot at sports events.

Yes, he's got that Australian tracksuit.
Yes, the one under his suit?

Yes.
Yes, I've got one on order. He's got a right-wing position on social issues like race and gender, sexuality.

You've got those pretty well now too.
I think the key is to keep expressing a concern for Australian families.

Yes, it's a great smokescreen, isn't it?
It's brilliant. No one knows what it means and I tell you what, when you do it, you can hear a pin drop.

I bet you can. You do it very well. You're very good at that. Have you ever met him, the real John Howard?
Yes, we bump into each other from time to time.

Does he like what you do?
He loves it.

He's a fan?
I saw him this week, Monday I think it was. It was in Adelaide.

What did he say?
He'd seen the thing I'd done on uranium.

Was he nice about it?
He said even he couldn't tell the difference.

High praise. That's great!
He actually congratulated me on it publicly, on Tuesday.

He did. You must be chuffed.
It doesn't get any better than 'I congratulate Mr Beazley on his courageous stand on the question of uranium'.

Mr Howard, thanks for your time.
Ha ha ha ha. Got you there, Bryan.

God, he's good.

Mr Andrews
A Concerned Parent

We knew he was working on something.

Mr Andrews, come in.
Thanks.

Please. Take a seat.
Is it about Kevin?

Yes.
I got your message. Is everything OK?

Well, we've just done a big project review. Are you aware of what Kevin was doing?
We knew he was working on something. There's a lot of clutter in the house.

It's to prepare them for the sort of task they might be asked to conduct as adults.
Yes, we understand that. It's great training. I don't know about Kevin's project in detail but I actually printed a lot of it out a work.

OK, just to put you in the picture, Kevin's taken on industrial reform.
Industrial reform?

You seem surprised.
Yes, don't know why he chose that. What would Kevin know about industrial reform?

I was going to ask you about that.
How did he go?

Well, I think he did a lot of work.
Yes, he did.

Look, to be honest he's got into trouble in a couple of key areas. Have a look.

(He reads.) Mmmm. Who are these companies?

They're all companies who don't wish to be associated with Kevin's project.

I'm not surprised. They're dependent on their staff, a lot of these companies. They'll go broke if they introduce…

I'm sure he thought he was helping them.

He hasn't thought this through though, has he? Did you talk to him about this? Has he had help with this?

Yes, I've spent a lot of time with Kevin.

Did he know these companies didn't want a bar of it?

Yes. He said that proved how good the proposal was.

Because these companies wouldn't wear it?

Yes.

Oh dear. *(He reads on.)* Oh God, and he's made it compulsory to dock your own workers' pay if they go to a meeting about it.

Yes, he's actually put them in a difficult position.

Couldn't the staff just say they're not coming in because they got pissed watching the soccer or they've got a pretend cold? Nobody would mind if they didn't come to work.

No, he's painted himself into a bit of corner.

It's all a bit of a mess, isn't it?

Imagine if this were happening in real life.

It'd be hopeless.

Can I ask you something? Is he happy, do you think? Kevin? Is he a happy kid?

I'd describe Kevin as a very normal kid.

Does he have any friends?
He doesn't relax easily socially, I have to say.

Has he ever mentioned John or Philip?
Yes. And Nick, he's got a friend called Nick.

Yes. Is he easily influenced?
This is not the Kevin we know. Is there something we can do at home?

He obviously thinks he's done pretty well with this project.
I think he thinks it's a triumph.

He might need some counselling.
Yes. I might take him camping for a couple of days. Get him out of the house.

Yes, move him round a bit.
Quite a lot I think. I might take the dog. *(He looks again at his son's work.)* Poor bugger. He tried so hard.

The Hon. Kevin Rudd
Leader of the Opposition

Am I going to give it a red-hot go?

Mr Rudd, thanks for your time.
It's very good to be with you, and thank you for the invitation.

Mr Rudd, you've announced your industrial relations policy this week. I just want to...
Yes, we have, Bryan. Do I think we're going to solve all of the problems in one go and do I think this is going to be popular with everybody? No I don't. But do I think it's a better, fairer, more equitable solution for all Australians, Bryan? Yes, I most assuredly do.

Good. Mr Rudd...
Do I think Industrial Relations and Workplace Relations are important, are of the utmost importance in this country? Is that my belief? Yes, it most emphatically is. Do I therefore assume that I am simply some sort of Robin Hood who can come along and solve all the problems of the world at a stroke, Bryan? I'll be brutally honest with you. I don't.

No.
No, that is not my view. But am I going to give it a go, Bryan? Am I going to give it a red-hot go? Yes, Bryan, that is my belief. That is my commitment. And that is the policy we will be taking to the Australian people.

Yes Mr Rudd...
We've dropped the ball in this country. We have seriously dropped the ball in this country. We've dropped the ball on global warming. We've dropped the ball on this absolutely ill-advised and doomed war in Iraq. Do I think it's going to be easy to get out of these things, Bryan? I don't.

Probably not, no.
No, I don't. But do I think the Australian public deserves a better
go than they're going to get from this bereft, idea-less Howard
government?

Probably, yes.
Absolutely right. Yes I do.

So Mr Rudd...
Let me ask *you* a question, Bryan. Are we in this country thoroughly
sick of being told what the agenda is and told what to think or, Bryan,
do we take the view that we're not children and we don't need to be
treated like children?

Yes. Yes we do. But this is not what I asked you, Mr Rudd.
Am I interested in what you ask me, Bryan? Do I look as if I'm
interested in what you ask me? Do I look as if I'm yearning for further
information about what you actually asked me? Bryan, if I were, I'd be
answering that question.

Mr Rudd.
And am I doing that? No, I'm not.

**Well, Mr Rudd, this is not the question I've asked you. I wanted to
ask you about the Australian Workplace Agreements.**
Sure. Are we leaving some of the AWAs in place for a very limited
period? Yes, we are.

(To someone off screen.) What do I do with this?
But do we like AWAs? Do we think they're fair? No, we most
certainly do not. If we don't think they're fair, why are we leaving them
in place, Bryan, for a limited period?

Well, that's a good question.
That's a *good* question. That's a very good question. I congratulate you
on the question. Am I going to answer the question? No I'm not. Is it
the right question? No it isn't.

Mr Rudd...

What is the right question? Bryan, that's a very good question. That's an even better question.

I can't do anything here.

Here's another question. Am I a conceited twerp? Bryan, that question is beneath you. You're better than that, Bryan.

Yes.

These are very, very good questions.

He won't shut up.

Very good questions. Should I shut up now? Perhaps I should. In what direction should I shut?

Up.

Correct. What's the capital of Norway?

Oslo.

You're very good, Bryan. Very, very good.

Mr Rudd, thanks for your time.

Oh thank you, Bryan. I loved it. There's nothing I like more than an exchange of ideas.

The Hon. John Howard
Prime Minister of Australia

When is this going to happen?

Mr Howard, thanks for your time.
It's a great pleasure to be with you.

I'd like to talk to you about global warming and climate change.
Global warming and climate change?

Yes, what is Australia doing about…
Hang on. (*He is writing it down.*) Global warming.

Global warming and climate change.
Global warming?

Yes, the globe is getting warmer.
When is this going to happen?

It's happening now…
Well, do you want to talk about that as well?

Yes, it's the same thing. Global warming means the globe is warming.
So that's still 'global warming'. We'll cover that under 'global warming' won't we?

Yes. Mr Howard, we've got rising sea-levels, climate change, Australia's one of the most affected places on earth.
Sorry, what was the other one. 'Global warming' and what?

Climate change.
(*Writes.*) 'Climate change?'

Yes. The climate is changing. We've just had the hottest October in donkey's years.
(*Writes.*) 'Climate change'.

It's urgent that we do something about all this.
Urgent?

Mr Howard it was urgent we do something about this ten years ago.
(*Writes.*) 'Urgent.'

Mr Howard...
Hang on, Bryan. How do you spell 'urgent'?

U r g e n t
Looks wrong.

It's right, Mr Howard.
(*Writes again.*) 'Urgent.'

Yes, Mr Howard, what is the Australian government doing to ensure that...
Bryan, I'm trying to get all this down so we can discuss it. 'URGENT.'
Yes. Looks better in capitals.

Mr Howard.
Right. Global warming. Climate change. And it's urgent.

It was urgent ten years ago.
Is it still urgent?

Yes.
We'll cover that under 'urgency'. Anything else?

No. Mr Howard, what is Australia doing about climate change and global warming?
Climate change and global warming?

Yes.
Hang on. I've got them the wrong way round. Is it still urgent?

Yes.
Can we have some water?

We haven't got any water.
Don't be silly, Bryan.

The Hon. Joe Hockey
Minister for Workplace Relations

I am after all the minister for WorkChances.

Mr Hockey, thanks for your time.
Good evening. Very nice to be with you on this excellent program of yours.

Are you still the minister for workplace relations?
Yes, I am, yes. That's right. You're fired.

So, Mr Hockey, you're aware of these findings about WorkChances aren't you?
WorkChoices.

WorkChoices, I'm sorry, I beg your pardon.
Yes, I am aware of the finding you mentioned. I am after all the minister for WorkChances.

WorkChoices.
Precisely. I am aware of the findings, Bryan.

Now, the director of the government's Workplace Authority...
Barbara Bennett.

Barbara Bennett, yes. She was in the government's ad campaign, right?
She was, yes, advertising the Fairness Test.

Now, there were a lot of people who said she shouldn't have been in those ads, of course.
She's not a bad choice, Bryan. She was running the Fairness Test. The advertisements are for the Fairness Test. She's an ideal choice to advertise the Fairness Test.

But who paid for the ads?
The government.

They were in favour of the Liberal Party policy.
Well, I don't want to worry you unduly here, but the Liberal Party is the government.

Same thing?
Same thing. They are essentially the same thing.

But you're aware that Barbara Bennett's...
I am aware, certainly, that she recently announced that 25,000 cases of agreements had been found by her to be unfair.

Yes, they failed the test. They failed your own fairness test.
They failed the Fairness Test, which is good.

It's good your own Fairness Test has failed?
Yes. That establishes that the Fairness Test works.

So you've been caught out by your own system?
What do you mean caught out, Bryan? The Fairness Test works.

Mr Hockey, the agreements aren't fair. You've introduced them. And 25,000 of them have been found to be unfair.
That's right. It's great. The Fairness Test works.

But they're not fair.
The system works, Bryan! The Fairness Test is designed to determine whether things are fair, it finds an astonishing incidence of unfairness, 25,000 of these agreements are unfair. The system works. Who put the fairness test there, Bryan? We did, of course.

Well, you did, you did. Of course you did.
It's highly successful.

If the Fairness Test has determined the system doesn't work, that 25,000 people are being treated unfairly under your own system...
Bryan, who put the Fairness Test there?

You did. You did.
Exactly. The system works.

Why were the unfair agreements written in the first place?
I think the employers in those 25,000 instances hadn't seen the ads.

Which ads?
The ones that Barbara Bennett did for us.

For the government or for the Liberal Party?
Same thing, Bryan.

Well, were the agreements fair?
The agreements? No, not in those 25,000 cases. That's what she's determined.

So what are you saying? They're made fair by being found to be unfair?
No, I'm not saying that. That would be completely illogical. What I am saying is that the system works.

Well, can we change the law under which they're written, Mr Hockey?
Change the law?

Yes.
Be reasonable, Bryan. What is Barbara Bennett going to do if we change the law? If we make the law fair, what's the possible point in having a fairness test? She runs the Fairness Test.

She'd lose her job.
Have some compassion, Bryan. We're talking about people.

Mr Hockey, thanks for your time.
I'm a people person.

Kevin the First

3 December 2007 – 24 June 2010

Just fucking do it. I'm not interested in excuses.
I told you to fucking do it yesterday. I told you
again this morning. I left a fucking message for
you explaining how to fucking do it. And have you
fucking done it? No, you fucking haven't. Now, it's
simple enough. Just fucking do it.

Kevin Rudd, good evening.
Good evening, Bryan.

Are you OK there?
Yes, just engaging in light colloquy with a member
of my staff.

Is it OK to talk now?
Yes.

The Hon. Kevin Rudd
Prime Minister of Australia

Great. Very stimulating. I love it.

Now Kevin, about next year.
Yes.

You're going to be head boy.
I am, aren't I? Yes.

Now look Kevin, I don't want to be critical. I think you've done a terrific job since John left the school.
Yes, I have. Yes.

But what do you think of your speech at prize-giving?
My speech? I thought it was good. I got a really good response.

It wasn't a bit long? We do try to keep this under two hours.
What, the speech night?

No, the speech.
Well, I had a lot to cover because it had been a busy year, and there were all the sports results and some of them were still coming in.

Sure. How are you finding the workload?
Great. Very stimulating. I love it. I love it.

That's good. And you've been on a school trip recently, haven't you?
Yes, we went on the environmental science outing up to Bali.

Did you enjoy that?
I loved it. Yes. Got my photo in the paper.

I saw that. And you spoke at it, didn't you?
I did. Yes.

Said you were going to do something about climate change.
I am.

What are you going to do about that?
I'm going to fix it.

When are you going to do that?
Urgently.

Urgently?
Yes.

Do you know when exactly? Because we're going to have to put it in the program.
Yes. Next year.

Urgently next year?
Yes, next year urgently.

Right. Do you know when next year, Kevin?
Yes, urgently. It's an urgent problem.

And are you working well with Julia?
Yes, Julia's great. I really like Julia.

She's very bright.
She is. She's great. Can I talk to you about Garrett?

Peter Garrett?
Yes.

Yes, sure, what about him?
Laryngitis.

He's got laryngitis?
Yes.

When?
Until I say so.

Right. I'll just make a note of that.
And have we got a forwarding address for John?

Yes. Has something come in for him?

I think it's a Christmas present or something. I don't know what it is.

Who is it from?

From Awb someone. Awb?

Awb? Oh AWB?

AWB someone.

Yes, that's right. John was doing a wheat project with Downer and young Vaile.

Oh, yes. Maybe you should get this to Brendan. Can you get it to Brendan?

Yes, just leave it here and I'll give it to him.

No, I wouldn't leave it here.

Why not?

It's ticking. It's a ticking gift.

(Off.) Nelson, headmaster's office now!

Is Nelson coming back next year?

Yes, I believe so.

I hope so. Because I really like him.

Really? He's not very nice about you.

I don't care. I like him.

What do you like about him?

He's not Turnbull.

You know, Turnbull's coming back next year.

Turnbull's coming back next year?

Yes.

I could drop this at Turnbull's house. I know where he lives. It's on my way home.

Why would Turnbull want something that's ticking and isn't addressed to him?
Good point. I'll gift-wrap it. Can you get me a bow?

You better put some chocolates in there, too.
And some choccies?

The Hon. Brendan Nelson
Leader of the Opposition

I'm beautifully positioned, Bryan.

Brendan Nelson, thanks for your time.
I can assure you, Bryan, that it is my pleasure always to talk to you and that I'm going to keep talking to you. I'm listening to you, too, during the brief interstices between the elements of my own discourse. I'm listening very intently to what you're saying to me.

Yes, Dr Nelson, how are things going?
Very, very well indeed, thank you.

Your popularity is up a bit and down a bit, isn't it?
Well, there's only a bit of it; it's probably good that it's moving about.

It might attract some attention.
Indeed, yes. But it's going well.

Yes, and now John Howard is helping?
And John Howard's announced now that he's going to help, which is just fantastic.

Dr Nelson, aren't you in enough trouble without John Howard helping you?
Oh no, it's fantastic that John is deciding to help.

But you talk about a lot of different issues, don't you?
Well, I have to speak about a lot of subjects. After all, I'm the prime minister.

Well, no you're not. You're the leader of the opposition.
At the moment. I mean, technically, I'm the leader of the opposition, but I'm beautifully positioned, Bryan. One out and one back.

So if Kevin Rudd's popularity falls...
If Kevin Rudd's popularity comes back maybe sixty, seventy per cent, watch me go, Bryan, I'm in.

Listen, don't take this the wrong way. In order to heighten your chances I've given you a list of some subjects I think you should try and avoid.
Some subjects I should avoid?

Yes, I'm just trying to help, you know. You're obviously a nice man.
I am a nice man, yes.

You seem like a nice man.
Well, I'm trying to seem like a nice man. 'Nice but tough' is actually the look I'm after.

Well, that's the way you come across.
Good. That seems to be going pretty well then.

There are a few subjects here.
OK. So keep off health, education, the economy, defence. Why keep off these matters?

Well, you can't mention these because you were in the previous government and you were associated with a lot of the decisions that the electorate rejected.
I stand by a lot of what we did in government. We were a fantastic...

You see, that is your difficulty—Dr Nelson, listen to me.
How could I not stand by what we did, Bryan? I was a crucial, one might almost argue an essential, pinion in that government.

Dr Nelson, you are not helping yourself here. For a start, you criticised Kevin Rudd for saluting George Bush.
'Conducting unbecoming,' I said. Rather well phrased, I thought.

Come on. He didn't go into an unnecessary war based on a whole pack of lies, a war that we can't get out of.
Well, I was thinking perhaps of defence more generally.

Who bought the Sea Sprite helicopters?
I see your point, Bryan. I take your point. It's a good point. But surely I can talk about the economy.

No, you can't. There are 200,000 people sleeping in doorways and parks at the moment.
Bryan, we were only in office for a decade!

People can't afford a house in this country.
We were only there for ten years.

You've got to stay off these subjects. You just look and sound ridiculous.
Well, what can I talk about? This list is ...

The ones on the back. Have a look on the back.
Pardon? Oh, OK.

We'll run through them, OK?
Yes.

All right. You ready?
Yes. Certainly.

Would you like a cup of tea?
Yes, thanks.

Milk?
Just a flash in the pan.

'Just a dash', I think it says.
Sorry, can't read the font. *(Mobile phone rings.)* Whoops! There's the phone.

Hang on, hang on, hang on. Don't answer it…
It'll be John. He's trying to help.

Don't answer it. Don't answer it.
Really?

Don't answer it.
(Whispers.) Sorry, John.

Kevin Rudd's Father
A Concerned Parent

We thought he must be sleeping at school.

Thanks for coming in.
That's all right. Is it about Kevin?

It is about Kevin but it's not all about Kevin.
Have you told Kevin that? I'm pretty sure he thinks it's all about…

I wanted to have this conversation with you first.
Is he going all right?

Kevin's going very well. We're very pleased with him.
He's very pleased with himself.

He should be. He's going well.
Yes he tells us he's going well.

When does he sleep, Kevin?
We don't know. We thought he must be sleeping at school.

No, he's not sleeping here. He came back from this geography trip and…
Yes, we're knee-deep in postcards.

And he ran a big conference.
Yes, he's very keen. He loves it.

Yes. Now, there's a boy here, a new boy, who's a bit lost.
That's no good.

He's maybe a bit out of his depth. Having trouble fitting in.
I'm sorry to hear that.

We wonder if Kevin could play a role here.
Yes, I'm sure he could. I'm sure he'd be good at it.

The boy's name is Brendan.
Oh Brendan? With the haircut?

Yes, I wonder if Kevin could take him under his wing a bit.
We know Brendan.

How do you know Brendan?
He comes home with Kevin sometimes. He follows him home. Kevin took him to the conference didn't he?

He did.
Yes. Kevin did his homework one night.

Did he? What homework?
Aboriginal history.

Yes, Brendan did quite well in that.
Yes he did.

He got second.
Yes. Kevin got first I think.

Yes he did. So you know Brendan?
Yes, we see him a bit. Kevin says Brendan's friends aren't very nice to him.

No, that's very perceptive of Kevin.
Brendan's imaginary friend is nice to him.

Brendan has an imaginary friend?
Yes.

And his imaginary friend is nice to him.
Yes.

Well, that's nice, if his real friends aren't being nice to him.
Yes, it's good.

And who is Brendan's imaginary friend?
Kevin.

Are you sure Kevin doesn't sleep at home?
No. He's always working on some project. He's just finished one.

What was it?
Governor-general. Beautiful new governor-general. Pink raffia work.

The Hon. Kevin Rudd
Prime Minister of Australia

You've basically got two columns.

Kevin Rudd, thanks for your time.
Good to be with you, Bryan.

You've got a $57 billion deficit.
Wayne Swan has had to frame probably the most important budget of recent times.

Malcolm Turnbull says he would have delivered a surplus.
And Malcolm's imaginary friend Joe Hockey says he would have delivered a deficit of $25 billion.

This is the biggest deficit in our history.
You don't want to be too frightened of the term, Bryan. It's just a word.

Deficit.
Yes, people do it all the time. Companies do it. Temporary deficit.

Temporary deficit.
Yes. They're just words.

So when are we coming out of the deficit?
2015–2020.

Six to ten years?
Six to ten temporary years.

What's a temporary year?
A year in which we have a temporary deficit.

Was the Second World War temporary?
I've seen this analogy. 1939–45. It's not still happening. Have you been out?

Yes, so where's the money coming from?
It comes from the other column. You've basically got two columns and if you've got an amount in one column you've got to have it in the other.

What if you haven't got the money?
You've got a deficit. That's what a deficit is. You're financing your budget with a deficit.

But where does the money come from?
From the other column.

What's the difference?
It's the difference between what you're spending and what you've got.

You've got a deficit?
Temporarily.

Temporarily for ten years?
It doesn't matter how long a temporary deficit lasts.

Why not?
Because it's temporary.

Mr Rudd, the other thing that happened during the week was the announcement that you're going to postpone doing anything about the environment until you've fixed the economy.
That's the responsible thing to do. And it's radically different from the Howard government's position. They didn't do anything about the environmental crisis at all.

You're not going to do anything about it either.
Yes we are. We've been very clear about our environmental policy. We've put a lot of work into it. It's a very well worked out, superior policy. We're committed to carbon reduction.

But you're not going to do it.
Yes we are.

When?
As soon as we fix the economy.

Have you let the environment know there's been a delay?
Have we let the environment know?

It would be a courtesy, wouldn't it? A phone call or something.
You can't just ring the environment. That's ridiculous.

You're saying you're better on the environment because the policy you're not going to bring in is a better policy.
It's significantly better.

Have you got a list of the other things you're not going to do? Why don't you solve world poverty?
Julia, have you got a pencil? Bryan's on a roll. Anything else you can be committed to because you're not going to do it?

You could cure all the world's diseases.
Oh, I've always wanted to not do that.

So when will you be doing it?
As soon as we possibly can't.

The Hon. Malcolm Turnbull
Leader of the Opposition

A dog ate it.

Malcolm, sit down. Are you OK?
Yes, I'm all right.

**What's happened, Malcolm? You were going along pretty well.
Is there a problem?**
No problem.

I don't see much evidence of anything much going on.
I'm doing stuff.

What are you doing?
Stuff.

**Malcolm, I'm giving you the opportunity to tell me what's gone
wrong.**
Nothing's gone wrong.

Something's gone wrong.
Nothing's gone wrong.

**Let me finish, Malcolm. It's not just me who thinks this. This is not
the Malcolm we've seen in previous years.**
Same Malcolm.

**Let me finish please, Malcolm. You're bright enough. You've got
access to all the help you want.**
I'm going along OK.

**Well, I don't know that you are. You're falling behind. You're way
behind some of the other boys.**
I'll catch up.

That's what you said in April. Where's your ETS homework? You were supposed to have handed in an outline for an Emissions Trading Scheme.

A dog ate it.

A dog ate it?
Yes.

What about your notes? Can't you go back to your notes?
A dog ate my notes.

The same dog?
Another dog.

Why haven't you come to us and explained that? You can't just not do anything.
I'm doing things.

What are you doing?
Can I have an extension?

You've had an extension. What happened to your last extension?
A dog ate it.

A dog ate your extension?
Yes.

Different dog, I suppose?
Yes. An extension-eating dog.

Malcolm, this doesn't even make sense. You've actually had three extensions. When is it due?
It was due months ago.

It was due in July.
A dog ate July.

A dog ate July?
Yes.

What was the dog's name?
Tuckey.

Senator Nick Minchin,
the Hon. Tony Abbott,
the Hon. Joe Hockey,
the Hon. Andrew Robb,
the Hon. John Howard,
the Hon. Peter Dutton,
the Hon. Malcolm Turnbull,
the Hon. Kevin Andrews,
the Hon. Ian Macfarlane,
Senator Steve Fielding

I like it better over here.

Nick Minchin, thank you for joining us.
Good to be with you, Bryan.

Tony Abbott, thanks for your time tonight.
Pleasure.

And Joe Hockey, good to see you.
Good to be with you, Bryan.

And Andrew Robb, thanks for your time.
Good evening.

And John Howard, thanks for coming in this evening.
Pleasure.

And Peter Dutton, too, thank you as well.
I can't find a seat. I'll be with you in a minute.

And Malcolm Turnbull, thanks for coming in.
Thank you.

Kevin Andrews, thanks for your time.
Good evening.

Tony Abbott, thanks for your time.
Good to see you, Bryan.

Haven't I just introduced you?
Yes. Happy to be here with you, Bryan.

Weren't you over there?
Yes, I shifted my position. I like it better over here.

OK. Well, thanks for coming in.
Pleasure, Bryan.

Ian Macfarlane, thanks for your time this evening.
Good to be here.

Nick Minchin, thank you for your time.
Good to be here, Bryan.

You were over there, too.
No, I was pretending to be over there. This is my real position here.

Senator Fielding. What are you doing here?
I've got to be here. I represent so many people that nothing can happen in the parliament without my approval.

How many people do you represent?
There's Dave and Beryl and Trevor.

No, don't go through and name them all. Just tell me how many there are.
Three.

Tony Abbott, good evening.
Good evening, Bryan.

What are you doing over here? You were over there.
Don't worry about where I might have been before. I'm over here now.

OK. Now we're here to discuss where the Liberal Party goes from here, and can I first come to you, Malcolm Turnbull?
Bryan.

Tony Abbott.
Can I point out I've got explosives strapped to myself and if I don't like the way this discussion is going I'm going to take this whole studio out.
Minchin: I've got explosives too.
Robb: So have I.
(Voices off camera.) So have I.
Abbott: We've all got explosives, Bryan. Don't get the idea we're not serious about this. We can take the building out.
Turnbull: Morons. I mean, really, Bryan, I've wasted enough time on these bozos.

I'll come with you.
(There is a loud explosion.)

What was that?
John: No idea. Keep walking.

A Federal Police Officer

Just stay behind that line, please.

Thanks for your time tonight.
Pleasure.

You're with the federal police?
I am.

What's your exact position?
As far as this current matter is concerned, I'm the incident controller.

OK. So can you tell us what happened?
Just stay behind that line, please.

I'm sorry. Can you tell us exactly what happened?
We'll be releasing a statement when we know exactly what's happened in every respect.

What can you tell us at the moment?
Not very much, I'm afraid. We're still gathering evidence at the scene.

Obviously there's been an incident.
An incident has occurred.

Can you tell us the nature of the incident?
An incident has occurred involving a number of male Caucasians.

Any female Caucasians involved?
Yes, female Caucasians are also believed to have had some involvement in the incident.

And some damage has occurred?
Damage has occurred, yes, as a result of the incident.

Structural damage?
Yes indeed. At this stage we believe an edifice has fallen over.

Were there people in it at the time?
There are certainly fears held for some of the persons who were believed to be in there at the time.

People have been hurt?
We have a number of persons currently being assessed by health professionals.

Do we have any idea yet as to how the incident started?
We have reports, unconfirmed, that a group of male Caucasians entered the edifice, from one door of the edifice, and another group of male Caucasians entered from another door.

Where were they from?
The first male Caucasian was from the Sydney area, but we have them from Victoria, and we have some who are known to the authorities in Queensland. We've even got one from Adelaide.

Then what happened?
There was a discussion about unity, and as a result a number of persons were injured.

Will arrests be made?
We have issued a statement. Let me read it to you. 'An incident has occurred at a location in the Canberra area. Substantial damage has resulted to a major edifice and engineers believe it may have to be completely rebuilt. A number of Caucasians are believed to have been involved in the incident, which caused an explosion, a fire, some damage to property, personal injury and approximately eighty persons were involved.'

Who was responsible?
There are no suspicious circumstances.

They did it themselves?
At this stage we believe no one else was involved.

It was some sort of cult thing?
We're not sure why it happened.

Is there a warning in this for the rest of the community?
Yes, we would say to anyone out there who is planning a gathering to discuss party unity, try to do it in a large open area and, for goodness sake, alert the fire brigade beforehand.

Thank you.
Pleasure.

How long will you be here?
I'll be here for a couple of days. There's still a lot of smouldering in there.

A Financial Consultant

A trillion each.

Your name is Roger?
Roger.

That's your name?
Roger.

And what do you do, Roger?
I'm a financial consultant.

A financial consultant?
Roger.

And how's business?
Not bad. We've had a bit of a quiet period lately.

What do you mean 'lately'?
Since the war.

OK. Your special subject is the economies of the European Community. Your time starts now. How much does Greece owe?
Two hundred and thirty-six billion dollars.

Correct. Who do they owe it to?
Other European economies.

Correct. How much does Ireland owe?
Eight hundred and sixty-seven billion dollars.

Correct. Who do they owe it to?
Other European economies.

Correct. How much do Spain and Italy owe?
A trillion each.

Correct. Who to?
Germany, France and Britain.

Correct. How are Germany, France and Britain going?
They're struggling.

Correct. Why?
They've got their money invested in these economies that can't pay it back.

Correct. So what are they going to do?
They're going to have to bail them out.

Correct. Where are they going to get the money to do that?
I don't know.

How much does Portugal owe?
Hang on, what was the answer to that last question?

Just keep answering the questions, Roger. Where is Portugal going to get the money it owes to Germany if it can't get back the money it's lent to Italy?
Hang on. The question was 'where are a lot of broke economies going to get the money to bail one another out?'

You're wasting valuable time, Roger. How much money does Spain owe to Italy?
Forty-seven billion, but where are they going to get it?

Correct. What does Italy owe to Spain?
Thirty-one billion but they're broke.

Correct. How can they pay each other if neither of them has any money?
They're getting a bailout.

Correct. Where's the money coming from for a bailout?
That's what I'm asking.

Correct. Why are people selling the European currency and buying the $US?
Because the US economy is stronger than the EU economies.

Correct. Why?
It's owned by China.

Correct. Very well done and after that round you've lost a million dollars.
I thought you said, 'Well done.'

Yes. Well done. You've only lost a million dollars. Extraordinary performance.

Julia Caesar

4 June 2010 – 27 June 2013

First woman leader. You must be very proud of that.
Well, I don't accept your premise there, Bryan. It's an honour to lead this nation. It would be an honour for anyone to lead this nation. This is a great nation.

Can you think of a woman leader before you?
Julia Caesar.

Julius **Caesar I think he was.**
Julia Caesar, Bryan. And Julia Lecter.

Duly elected isn't really a person's name.
You haven't allowed me to complete that statement, Bryan. Duly elected I will, of course, review all the ministries and the policies and the programs. I'll do this in a consultative way.

You'll ring Bill Shorten?

The Hon. Julia Gillard
Prime Minister of Australia

A good government but it had lost its way.

Julia Gillard, thanks for your time tonight.
It's my pleasure to be here, Bryan.

First, congratulations on becoming prime minister.
Thank you.

It's all happened very quickly, hasn't it?
It has. These things are never easy, on anyone, on Kevin, on the government, on the Australian people, and it was important in this instance that we resolve matters quickly and get on with the business of managing the country.

Yes, and you've announced a relatively unchanged cabinet.
Last Thursday I said, and I still say, the government was a good government but it had lost its way.

You need to find that way?
We need to find a way, not necessarily that same way. I think we had lost some direction. We needed clarity, we needed agility and we needed certainty. Those are the elements I have sought to put in place as quickly as possible.

Yes, have you had time to take it all in, what it's going to mean for you personally?
Oh look, Bryan, I've been in politics for a while and I understand the media are always interested in the personal details but the main thing here is to get the best result for Australian workers, for the very important resources sector, for education and health and for the environment.

First woman leader, though. You must be very proud of that.
Well, I don't accept your premise there, Bryan. It's an honour to lead this nation. It would be an honour for anyone to lead this nation. This is a great nation.

Can you think of a woman leader before you?
Julia Caesar.

***Julius* Caesar I think he was.**
Julia Caesar, Bryan. And Julia Lecter.

Duly elected isn't really a person's name.
You haven't allowed me to complete that statement, Bryan. Duly elected I will, of course, review all the ministries and the policies and the programs. I'll do this in a consultative way.

You'll ring Bill Shorten?
Bryan, I'm not going to canvass the large number of individuals and bodies, be they corporate or be they departmental, with whom I'll be having discussions over ensuing days, weeks, month and years. It's too early to be doing that.

Do you accept that you've been put there by the faceless men of the ALP faction system and that you're in debt to those powerbrokers?
No I don't, Bryan. They're not faceless men. I know the media likes to portray things in that way but they have faces. That's how we recognise them. They're all elected members of the parliament and like Nick Minchin and the faction who installed Tony Abbott as leader of the opposition, they are simply trying to get the best result, electorally, for the party.

Were they right in Tony Abbott's case?
Bryan, I'm not going to canvass with you the decision the Australian people have to make. That is a matter for them. They have to decide whether they want to live in a country run by medievalists and flat-earthers and people-haters or whether they want to work with us, in a consultative way, on twaddle in some cases...

Twitter.
On Twitter in some cases, for the best result for Australian workers, for the very important resources sector, for education and health and for the environment.

But 'game on' you've said.
I have said that, Bryan.

And you mean it, obviously?
My judgment, Bryan, is that the way to express what I mean is to say it.

Thanks for your time tonight.
Good on you, Bryan.

The Hon. Tony Windsor and the Hon. Rob Oakeshott

You asked us both a question.

Tony Windsor, thanks for your time.
Pleasure.

And Rob Oakeshott, thanks for your time.
Pleasure.

Can I ask you both first, do you expect this government you've been party to installing to go full term?
Well, that's difficult to say in the case of this government, just as it is in the case of any government, and it's unlikely that if this government *doesn't* go full term, that it would be the independents who caused the problem because it's in our interests for the government to work. That's why we put it there the way we did.

Hang on, you're both talking together.
Pardon?

You're both talking together.
You asked us both a question.

I didn't mean for you both to answer me at the same time.
You did ask both of us.
I think maybe he meant 'Can I ask each of you'.
Yes, he did say 'Can I ask both of you'.
I know he did.

I did mean, 'Can I ask each of you?'
That's not what you said.

Maybe not, but it's what I meant.
If you're not going to say what you mean, how can you blame us if we don't understand you?

Don't look at me. He asked you the question.
Actually, I asked the question.
Wasn't as good as his question.

Look I'll explain how this works. I ask the questions. You answer them.
Have you done this sort of work before?

I've been doing it for twenty years.
Fair enough.
Maybe try another one.

You haven't answered my first one.
You've already said it wasn't what you meant.
Have you got something else there?

Right. I would like to know how long do you think this government will last?
Who are you asking?

Both of you.
We hope it lasts as long as possible.

Not together?
Do you mean 'each of you?'

I just wanted to get you both to answer the question.
Separately?

Of course, separately.
I hope the government goes full term.
So do I.

So you think the same thing?
On that issue we do.

Look either you've got the same view about everything or you don't.
That's right.

Well, which?
We don't.

You have so far.
So far you've asked one question.

Is this the new paradigm?
Who are you asking?

Both of you.
Do you mean either of us?

Yes. Does either of you think this is the new paradigm?
Yes.

Yes what?
Yes, I do.
Yes, he does. He told me earlier.

Maurits, A Quiz Show Contestant

Is it part of Australia or not part of Australia?

Your name is Escher.
Yes.

A surname, Escher?
That is my surname. My first name is Maurits.

OK, Maurits, and your special subject is asylum seekers.
People seeking asylum *in Australia*.

People seeking asylum from overseas in the Australian mainland.
Or in the outlying islands. Australia has quite a few islands, mainly to the north where a lot of people might arrive if they're coming from that direction.

By boat?
By boat, yes

Most of them would be coming from the north, wouldn't they?
Yes, that's why I make the point.

But haven't some of the islands been excised?
What do you mean 'excised'?

Well, Christmas Island, for example, has been made not part of Australia?
By whom?

By Australia. By the government of Australia.
So who would make a decision about procedural matters in relation to anything that happened there?

Australia would.
So is it part of Australia or not part of Australia?

Maurits, I'm really supposed to ask the questions here.
I just want to clarify what they're about.

That's what I'm trying to do. It says here 'Asylum seekers entering Australia'.
It says 'People seeking asylum in Australia'.

OK, but not seeking asylum in parts of Australia that Australia has decided aren't parts of Australia?
But which it still runs.

No. Australia can't be running things it doesn't run.
So who runs them?

Listen, Mauritz I'm going to start your actual questions now. We've got a lot to get through, OK? What is the legislation that covers the procedure for dealing with asylum seekers?
The Migration Act.

Correct. And what happens if they arrive at Christmas Island?
They would be covered by the Parts of Australia That Are Not Parts of Australia Act.

Correct. So who deals with people who land there?
That would be a decision made by the immigration minister.

Correct. Of which country?
Of Australia.

Correct. Why?
The country it's not part of is Australia.

Correct. There was a High Court decision about this recently. What did the High Court decide?
They decided they were the High Court of Australia and the parts of Australia that are not parts of Australia.

Correct. They've got to be, don't they? These questions are very confused. *(Looks off.)* Phil? Did you write these? They're very confused.

Have you got them up the right way?

They're the same up the other way.

They are too. Isn't that clever!

A Voter

I didn't throw out the previous prime minister.

Thanks for your time this evening.
Pleasure.

You're a voter?
Yes.

Have you seen the papers lately?
Yes, I read the papers.

Fine mess you've made of this whole thing, in my view.
What whole thing?

I presume you've seen the way things are going in this country?
We've got some problems, sure.

We certainly have. Are you happy now?
What do you mean, am I happy now?

You've put a pretty rickety old government in power, haven't you?
It wasn't just me.

Bits of it flying off. Bit of a deal with the independents here, bit of an arrangement with the Greens there. All held together with bits of Sellotape.
This is politics surely. These are just the forces of political argument being played out.

It's a bloody mess and you know it is.
I didn't say it wasn't a bit of a mess, but I'm not the only person who voted.

Let's have a look at what you've done here. You've put a prime minister in office who is less popular than the man she replaced.
I didn't throw out the previous prime minister.

Why was he thrown out at all?
He wasn't popular enough.

Wasn't popular enough?
That's right.

So he's been replaced by someone who is less popular? That doesn't even make sense.
I didn't do it. I'm just describing to you what happened.

I suppose you just woke up one morning and were told we had a new prime minister?
Yes.

One you hadn't voted for?
One who was voted for by the people who'd been elected into power.

By voters?
Yes.

There's a pattern emerging, isn't there?
You can't blame voters for this. It's compulsory to vote.

You've got a leader of the opposition who is less popular than the man he replaced.
We didn't do that either.

And why was he replaced?
The previous leader of the opposition?

Yes?
He had a policy.

What have they got now?
They've got a different leader.

He was elected, I suppose?
Yes. By party members.

Same pattern. Who's Paul Howes?
Can I have a glass of water?

Do you know a bloke called Nick Xenophon?
Nick Xenophon is a senator from South Australia. Why?

He wants me to call him.
What for?

Can I do a birthday party on Saturday?
Whose birthday is it?

Mine.
He's good.

A Health Professional

Quite a big sample group in the Canberra area.

Thanks for joining us.
Pleasure.

You're issuing a general health warning.
We don't want to be alarmist. Can I say to people, it's more of an awareness program?

OK. What seems to be the problem?
We think it's a virus. The difficulty from an epidemiological point of view is the extent of it.

It's obviously been difficult to diagnose.
No, but we're now seeing it in patients we've never seen it in before.

And what does that mean?
It means that what we thought was a natural immunity isn't protecting people anymore.

And where have you done the study?
This comes from quite a big sample group in the Canberra area. We've seen it there before but previously only in about half the population.

Now it's everywhere?
Yes.

And where else is it?
Everywhere else.

Yes?
Both places.

And what is it?
Coalitionitis. How technical can I get? It causes an inflammation of the pericompromise.

What's that?
It's the fibrous sac in which the policy gland sits.

I see.
And that then puts pressure on the gland itself.

Glands secrete, don't they?
They do. And if you put extra pressure on that gland…

…it secretes more?
It'll secrete anything.

To relieve the pressure?
Yes.

What are the symptoms? What should people look for?
Headaches, fever, muscle pain.

Can you go a bit green?
You can.

I think I've seen this. You said fifty per cent of the sample group have always had the condition?
That's right.

Are they immune?
No, they're carriers. They've got the disease.

So they've had it for a while. And what do they do?
If you've had it for a while you can find yourself saying things you don't believe.

Do you contradict yourself?
Yes and no.

And this is happening in Canberra?
Yes. It's isolated in that area at the moment.

So it shouldn't affect anyone else?
No, it will affect people all over the place.

Why?
That's where they come from.

These viri?
Yes. They're flying in formation up there.

Con, A Quiz Show Contestant

Their policy is to remain in government.

Your name is?
Con.

I suppose your surname is 'Fused'?
Fused? No. My surname is Vergence.

Con Vergence?
Con Vergence.

OK. Your special subject is Australian government policy on emissions trading?
Yes.

What is an emissions trading scheme?
A market-based impost which operates as an incentive to reduce carbon emissions.

Correct. In the Australian parliament, who is in favour of a market-based carbon price?
The government and Malcolm Turnbull.

Correct. And who is opposed to it?
The rest of the opposition.

Correct. So a market-based carbon price is the policy of the party in government?
No, it's not. They just want to bring it in.

Correct. And is a carbon tax the policy of the party of which Malcolm Turnbull is a member?
No, it's not. He's just in favour of it.

Correct. If Malcolm Turnbull doesn't agree with opposition policy, why isn't he a member of the government?
No one would notice him in there. He wouldn't stand out.

Correct. Why not?
All the members of the government are in that position.

Can you be a bit more specific?
Yes. All the members of the government are in favour of a policy that's
not the policy of their party.

Correct. If it's not their policy, why do they want to bring it in?
Their policy is to remain in government.

Correct. And how do they do that?
By bringing in a market-based price on carbon.

Correct. Why?
Because the people they need to talk to, to stay in government, are all
in favour of a carbon price.

**Correct. And what is the opposition's argument against a carbon
price?**
Their argument is that they should be the government.

Correct. Why aren't they the government?
Because they wouldn't bring in a carbon price.

Correct. Why are people confused about the carbon price?
Because the government hasn't explained it properly.

**Correct. If the government doesn't explain the carbon price, how can
people find out what it is?**
By listening to Malcolm Turnbull and the Greens.

Correct. Why don't the media ask them to explain it?
They're covering the fight between the government and the opposition.

Correct. And what is the fight about?
Whether a boiled egg should be broken at the big end or the little end.

Correct. And after that round you've won a compensation payment.
What for?

For the carbon tax.
What does that mean?

Correct.

Another Health Professional

Nobody forced them to go into the parliament.

Thanks for your time tonight.
Pleasure.

You're a health professional?
Yes, although you probably ought to be talking to the minister.

Well, I wanted to talk about the footage that's emerged this week of the psychological damage being done to these people who have been confined, sometimes for very long periods.
Yes, I work in this area.

It's shocking.
It is. This is not new to us. We've been saying this for some time.

Something should have been done about it well before this.
Yes, although resources are very stretched.

We're seeing anxiety problems, substance abuse, emotional issues, self-harm in some cases.
Terrible.

It's a real problem, isn't it. It's an indictment on the way we're doing things.
We can only do what's possible.

The main issue, surely, is these people's health.
It is.

It doesn't matter what we think of them. We owe them a duty of care.
That's right.

You work in this area. Tell us what conditions are like.
They've put themselves in this position.

What do you mean?
They've been elected. Nobody forced them to go into the parliament.

No, but once they're in there, surely they can be processed faster than this. Some of them have been there for years.
We make them as comfortable as we can.

In Canberra?
Yes, in Canberra, but they've got access to the outside world. There are phones and things.

In some cases they obviously don't know what's going to happen to them.
This is part of the problem. There's an impermanence about the whole experience.

And they must realise the damage they're doing.
I think a lot of them do, yes. A lot of them are Christians.

So there'd be a lot of guilt?
There is a lot of guilt. And a lot of denial.

Look at what they're doing to asylum seekers, for example.
Exactly.

They'd be blaming each other too, wouldn't they?
Oh yes. You can't get anyone to own up about anything.

Would they assimilate into society?
Some might. But some of them are institutionalised. There's a bloke in there, thinks he's Napoleon. There's a woman who listens only to small rodents.

But they can get help.
We're doing what we can.

Is there a long-term solution?
If you'd asked me this twenty years ago I'd have said yes.

What would you say now?
I've just told you what I'd say now.

It's tragic, isn't it?
It's appalling.

The Hon. Wayne Swan
Treasurer of Australia

Dane Swan? Who's Dane Swan?

Wayne Swan, thanks for your time.
Pleasure.

You're not going to believe this.
Try me.

I've got the wrong questions for this interview.
That might not be a bad thing from my point of view.

It's annoying. I had them both sitting there. I've picked up the wrong ones.
Are you sure? You seem to have plenty of questions.

I do but they're not for you.
It says Swan.

It does, but it's not you.
That's me. Wayne Swan.

Dane Swan. I'm interviewing Dane Swan tomorrow and these are his questions.
Dane Swan? Who's Dane Swan?

Dane Swan? He's a famous footballer.
Oh, I see.

He won the award this week for being the best.
I won an award this week for being the best.

Really? What were you best at?
I was presented an award for being the world's best treasurer.

Really?
Yes, we got through the GFC pretty well and that was recognised by these people in Europe.

Isn't the reason we came through the GFC so well principally to do with our mining industry?
Management of the economy. Sure, commodities have been in strong demand for a lot of the period.

But you need management at the national level?
That's what's being recognised.

Even though you're really a miner?
I'm not a miner. I'm a treasurer.

Yes, but perhaps these people see you as a sort of miner/treasurer.
The point I'm making is that since I've won an award too, perhaps some of these questions will work.

We could give them a try.
Yes.

How's your knee?
Good, thanks.

No trouble from the hammy?
No.

I did hear something about a niggle in the glutes.
No. Kevin's a problem in that area, but fine otherwise, thanks.

What did you think of your kicking on Saturday?
Nobody likes being kicked.

Anything else you'd like to say?
No, I was happy with the four points.

Thanks very much and good luck.
Thanks.

The Hon. Tony Abbott
Leader of the Opposition

No.

Tony Abbott, thanks for your time. I presume you've been at the big economics forum in Brisbane this week?
No.

You haven't? I thought you'd been at it.
No.

You haven't been there at all?
No.

Really? Were you invited?
No, I wasn't.

Wouldn't you have been invited?
No.

As opposition leader? Are you sure you weren't invited?
No.

No, you're not sure, or no you weren't invited?
No, that's right.

OK. But presumably you're aware of what's coming out of that forum about the economic outlook?
No.

You're not aware. You haven't been following the discussion about Australia's economic outlook?
No.

Are you interested in Australia's economic outlook?
No.

It's going pretty well, isn't it? The Australian economy?
No.

It's one of the best performing economies in the world, isn't it?
No.

Mr Abbott, do you realise you're answering all these questions in the negative?
No.

Is this something you decided to do? Just say 'no' to everything?
No.

Maybe you're not aware you're doing it. Has anyone pointed out to you that that's what you're doing?
No, they haven't.

Because you do it a lot, don't you?
No.

OK. Tony Abbott, is your name Tony Abbott?
No.

It's not?
No.

OK. You're just saying no to everything. Let me try something else. Would you deny that you're Tony Abbott?
No.

Do you disagree that the Australian economy is one of the most successful in the world at the moment?
No.

Would it be unreasonable to suggest that saying no to everything militates against developing a proper argument?
No.

Are you opposed to the view that this is why you haven't presented the public with any policies?
No.

Mr Abbott, thanks for your time. Would you like a cup of tea?
No.

Would it be false to suggest you'd like a cup of tea?
No.

And that you wouldn't like milk?
No.

Or that you couldn't indicate your preference for sugar with your hand?
(Holds up two fingers.)

A Financial Advisor

A thousand gold medals.

Thanks for your time tonight.
Pleasure.

You're a financial expert.
No, I'm a financial advisor.

What's the difference?
A financial advisor provides financial advice.

What does a financial expert do?
I don't know I'm afraid. I'm a financial advisor.

OK. Now, it was announced today that you're advising the Australian Olympic Team.
Yes, I've been asked to advise the team on aspects of the approach to the London games, yes.

Not long to go now before the Olympics.
They start in a day or so.

What advice can you give?
Well, there are several products.

Products?
Yes, Australia wants to do well at the Olympics. National prestige, etc.

All countries want to do well at the Olympics.
We've got plenty of products.

What products?
Here's one. Under this plan we would advance the Australian Olympic Team, say, a thousand gold medals.

There aren't a thousand events.
The events are another matter. Don't worry about events. I'm talking medals. We advance the team a thousand gold medals and then they can pay us back from the gold medals they actually win.

They won't be able to pay you back. There aren't a thousand events to win.
They can pay us back over time.

But they can't. There aren't a thousand gold medals.
Yes, there are. We've just advanced them a thousand gold medals.

There aren't a thousand events.
Look. How many medals is Australia expected to win at the London Olympics?

Ten?
See? You're well on your way with the payments.

Why can't we just be happy with the ones we've actually earned?
You'll slip well behind the rest of the world.

We'll slip behind who?
The sporting countries will eat you alive. Greece, Spain, Portugal, Italy, the US.

How many medals are they winning?
Greece is winning 10,000, Italy's going very well, 60,000 gold medals.

How are they going to pay it back? That's ridiculous.
Iceland. Quite a small population Iceland, but 42,000 gold medals.

How many is America winning?
They make their own. The Americans and the Chinese make their own medals.

Doesn't that debase the currency?
Not as long as they keep doing it, Bryan.

Why?

So there are enough gold medals to go around and these other people can pay back the medals they've borrowed.

But it is not based on anything.

I'm not suggesting this is going to end happily. I'm just trying to explain how it works.

Thanks for your time.

Pleasure.

Are you going to the Olympics?

I'll be there for the foreclosing ceremony.

A Storyteller

People love a story.

Thanks for your time this evening.
Pleasure.

You must be very pleased with the way the show is going.
Very pleased.

Great story.
Fantastic story.

Are you surprised by how well it's going? I suppose this sort of thing has always worked, hasn't it?
It has. But it hasn't been done in this form before.

And there are differences with the way you're telling it this time, aren't there?
Yes. This is multi-platform. It's on television, radio, very big on radio, it's in print.

And it's online as well?
It is.

OK. Let's talk about the story. Because it's a pretty compelling narrative isn't it?
It is and people love a story.

Right. So there's this small community and there's a woman and she's said to be a witch.
That's right.

And she's tried. Well, no, it's not what we would call a trial, is it?
No, in a trial you have evidence and that evidence is interrogated and there's proper process.

So what happens in this case?
This is just a drama.

Yes, but she's publicly accused, isn't she?
She's publicly accused and there's a list read out of all the things she's
being blamed for.

Plagues of snakes and things?
Everything they don't like, the weather.

Yes, and they bring forth evidence.
No, these people are just accusing her.

Accusing her of being a witch?
Yes.

But what's their evidence?
Her friends are all gypsies and thieves and fornicators.

Her friends are?
Yes. She's morally tainted. Apparently she used to work somewhere.

And what about her accusers? Are they pure?
It's not about them. They're the accusers. The focus is all on her.

Because she's a witch?
Yes, she's the one who's a witch.

She's being accused of being a witch?
That's right.

But why are they accusing her of being a witch?
Because she's a witch.

Is she actually a witch?
Well, no, there aren't any witches.

She's just a normal person?
Yes.

And they're trying to demonise her?
Yes.

But there's no evidence.
No, but they're accusing her very loudly. It's hard to ignore. You've seen it.

I have. It's really effective.
They've got this huge loudhailer and they wheel this thing out and accuse her through that.

It's loud.
It's deafening. You can't hear anything else. *(Voices off camera can be heard saying 'She's a witch'.)*

There they go.
(Picks up phone.) Do we know anyone in Salem?

A Cycling Administrator

I saw a Belgian once having breakfast.

Thanks for your time tonight.
Good to talk to you.

You've been involved in International Cycling Administration for some years?
Yes, I've been on the Board of Velocipedes International and Local.

The V.I.A.L.?
Yes.

Vial?
That's right.

This crisis that's occurring in world cycling must be having a devastating effect on the sport.
It is. Cycling will change. This is big. This is a huge thing.

How long has this drug-taking been going on? Twenty years?
Something like that.

You didn't know it was going on at all, did you?
We had no idea. We had no idea.

You must have attended the Tour de France.
I did. Every year.

You must have seen these cyclists every day during the tour?
I did.

You must have fraternised with them at night.
I did. I knew a lot of them personally.

But you had no idea any of them were using drugs?
No idea.

What did you think when you saw them riding up mountains at astonishing speeds?
I was astonished. I said so. I said 'this is astonishing'.

You didn't wonder why they were able to do that?
They were the best road cyclists in the world. This is what they're supposed to do.

You were never aware of any use of illicit substances at all?
Never. I had no idea. No idea.

You never saw anyone do anything unusual?
I saw a Belgian once having breakfast.

But you never saw anything else?
Never. I had no idea. No idea.

Were you aware they uses bikes?
I'd heard that, I'll be honest. But I'd never seen it myself.

What will happen now with the tour?
Well, we've got to clean up the sport.

And who will do that?
We will. Velocipedes International and Local.

Vial?
Yes, we've got to fix the sport. We've already changed our phone number.

Well, I hope you can do something about it.
We have to. The sport has been tarnished. We've got to rehabilitate an entire sport here.

Thanks for your time.
He says some of the riders are using bikes. I had no idea.

A Psephologist

It might be an idea to cook something.

Thanks for your time.
A pleasure to be here, Bryan, and can I congratulate you on getting
your own show?

It's not really a show.
It is and it's long overdue. I think you deserve it.

Thanks. Now the election has been called...
Are you going to sing and stuff? Move about a bit? You move well.

**No. I'll be talking to prominent people in politics and public life,
sport, the arts and so on.**
Have you got a desk? The other ABC shows have all got desks.

I don't need a desk.
You want to be taken seriously. I'd get one. Who's on your panel?

No, there isn't a panel.
How are you going to get off the point without a panel?

I won't be getting off the point.
Risky. Have you thought this through? Do you cook?

No, I won't be cooking.
It might be an idea to cook something. A boiled egg or just a bit of
steam drifting in from time to time. And then at the end you say 'we've
been cooking an egg this week and here's how you do it.'

You get an egg and boil it.
You see. You can cook.

Now. You're a psephologist?
That's right.

You study psephs?
We study electoral data.

You're going to be very busy this year, aren't you?
We are. We'll have a bumper crop this year.

What's the position as we enter what is really a very long campaign?
Well, the government has a majority of one. And it's a coalition government made up of the Labor Party and the independents and the Greens.

The opposition is a coalition too, of course.
It is. Of the Liberal Party and the National Party.

And what are going to be the key electorates to look at as things develop?
The danger areas for the government are Queensland, New South Wales and Western Australia, Victoria, Tasmania and South Australia and the territories.

Everywhere?
They're the main areas where they're in trouble.

Everywhere. What about the opposition? In what areas are they in trouble?
Policy, credibility, consistency and logic.

Everything?
It's pretty evenly balanced at the moment.

The government's had some problems just in the last week, hasn't it?
Well, the Obeid hearing in Sydney hasn't been doing them any good.

And the Craig Thomson charges can't have done them any good.
Yes, and there might be more charges there.

Really?
Yes, there are several laws under which Craig Thomson hasn't been charged with any offences at all.

Like what?

He hasn't been charged under the law of adverse possession. He hasn't been charged with behaving seditiously on a horse.

Currency offences?

Nothing about the rouble at all.

So there's plenty of fun ahead?

Yes, good, solid, marginally depressing Australian media song and dance.

Thanks for your time.

Failing to display a lamp on his ice-cream. They might have him there.

A Marketing Executive

Whatever truth you've got, we'll enhance it.

Thanks for your time tonight.
Pleasure to be with you.

You're in marketing?
Marketing is rather a broad term. We're really in brand management, product maximisation strategies and truth enhancement.

Truth enhancement. How can you enhance the truth?
What truth?

You said you work in truth enhancement. Doesn't that suggest you're dealing with the truth?
We hope so.

Yes. How can you enhance the truth?
What truth?

Any truth.
Whatever truth you've got, we'll enhance it.

But what's better than the truth?
Anything's better if it's enhanced. That's what enhanced means.

Well, what does truth mean?
Whatever it means, it can only be better if it's enhanced.

OK, now, we've got an election. Both parties are in full campaign mode.
Yes, they are indeed.

Both of them are pushing family values.
Yes. They're competing for very similar ground.

What are family values?
A set of values that holds the family as the basic social unit. Putting the family first. Parents maybe going without…

To give their children opportunities?
Yes.

Sacrificing?
Parents making sacrifices, yes, for their kids.

How are the parties going to get their message out to asylum seekers?
I don't think asylum seekers are the demographic the parties are after.

What could be more family values than risking your life to bring your children out of persecution and sectarian violence and give them a new start in a new country?
Yes, of course, many of us are the beneficiaries of courageous antecedents who did exactly that, but to answer your marketing question, there's no point in appealing to asylum seekers before the election.

Why not?
They don't get a vote.

So why is the government spending a fortune advertising to them?
In what way?

Huge full-page adverts in the paper telling them that if they try to get to Australia they're going to be taken to Papua New Guinea.
What language are the ads in?

In English.
Why would the government be advertising to asylum seekers in a language a lot of them don't understand in Australian newspapers they don't read?

Yes, that's the question.

The answer is I don't know. Perhaps the ads aren't really for asylum seekers.

Who are they for?

Maybe they're for people who live in Australia.

And who are thinking of leaving Australia and trying to get into Australia?

There mightn't be too many of those.

No.

Maybe the ads are for people who own newspapers.

Why would the government want to benefit media owners?

No, that can't be right.

Why have the lights gone out?

Hello.

A Media Commentator

Most Australians are media commentators.

Thanks for your time tonight.
Pleasure.

You're a media commentator?
I am, yes. Most Australians are media commentators.

This is a pretty dynamic time isn't it, in the media?
It is. It's partly the time of year of course; there are new shows like yours.

It's not really a show.
Yes, it is and it's rating its freckle off.

I meant the industry. Some channels are really struggling, aren't they?
That's right. It's a pretty tough market out there.

And what are the big shows?
It's still all reality television.

What is reality television?
It's where you get normal people and you put them in situations they wouldn't normally be in.

And you film it?
Yes.

In what sense is that reality?
It's not. It's reality television.

None of this would be happening if television hadn't created it.
That's right.

You said it was reality television.
Yes, it's reality television.

But you say it's not reality.
No. It's not reality. It's reality television.

Can you give me an example?
MKR is an example. TSI. WSS.

And what are they?
MKR. *My Kitchen Rules*, a series of shows that is effectively a cooking competition.

Why are there so many cooking shows?
It's a licence requirement in Australian television.

And what's TSI?
The Test series in India. This is a series of cricket matches between Australia and India.

Yes, India just won the second Test.
That's right. India scored *(Reads.)* 503.

What did Australia score?
Have you got a magnifying glass? I can't read this.

And what's WSS?
That's a new one. *Western Suburbs of Sydney*. They take some politicians and they put them in the western suburbs of Sydney.

And what do they do?
They walk about, they shake hands with people.

Where?
A fruit and vegetable shop. Nepalese takeaway.

And they film it all?
It's all filmed.

And then what happens?
At the end of the series the public votes.

And whoever gets the most votes wins the series?
And they get to run the country.

Don't the media run the country?
No, the person who wins the series gets to run the country.

Who won it last time?
A guy called Tony Windsor won it last time.

But the media are running the show, aren't they?
Yes, but the winner gets to run the country.

And the prize is awarded by the media?
It is.

Is Tony Windsor in it this year?
He is but he won't win this year.

How do you know that?
Why do you think they're doing it in Western Sydney?

I've got no idea.
I'm with you there, Bryan.

Thanks for your time.
Couldn't agree more.

His Eminence George Pell

You haven't asked the right question.

Cardinal Pell, thanks for your time tonight.
It's good to be with you.

You appeared this week before the Inquiry into the Handling of Child Abuse by Religious and Other Organisations?
I did. And, as I said to the members of the committee, I apologise for any wrong that may have been done. I'm aware that...

I don't think anybody doubts that the church is apologetic.
Do not interrupt. Just don't do it. I had this trouble with the committee.

That's probably because you weren't answering the question.
Do you have a question?

Yes.
I suggest you ask it.

What is the capital?
Oslo.

Can I complete the question?
I've given you the answer.

I'm afraid it's not the answer.
It is the answer.

What I was going to ask was 'What is the capital of Honduras?' It's not Oslo.
No, it isn't.

That's right.
In that case you haven't asked the right question, have you?

I've asked the wrong question?
Yes. I've given you the answer.

You've given me the answer you're prepared to give.
And you've asked me the question you're prepared to ask.

But you haven't answered the question.
It wasn't the right question.

You think you're handling all this pretty well, don't you?
I'm doing the best I can. We've got things wrong. That's what I'm
apologising for.

**Cardinal Pell, among the things that don't appear to be contested
is that records were changed to protect priests who had committed
crimes.**
Allegedly committed crimes.

No, they'd committed crimes. That's why they were being moved.
Where were they being moved to?

To places where they could commit other crimes.
I don't accept that.

You should do. You're apologising for the effects of it.
Let me explain something. We've got a problem and we need to fix it.
When I was in Rome recently I spoke to senior officials and they are
very keen about cleaning this whole situation up.

**Where were you staying in Rome? You were staying in the house the
church bought for $30 million.**
That's an observation and not a very useful one.

What were you doing in Rome?
I was attending a conference on poverty.

Do you think this issue is going to cost the church a lot of money?
Yes. That's up to others and we've said we'll abide by their decisions.
Can I ask you a question?

Yes.
Are you a Cath—

—no, I'm not.
Hang on, I haven't finished the question.

In that case the question was wrong.
How do you know?

I've never been a Catherine Zeta-Jones fan.
She was very good in *Chicago*.

She was good in *Chicago*.

A Pollster

We just cover things.

Thanks for your time tonight.
Good to be here, Bryan. Love your show.

Thanks. It's not really my own show.
Well, it wouldn't work very well without you.

OK. You're a pollster. This is what you do for a living.
A polster?

Yes.
Yes, that's what we do.

You've had a busy time lately.
We're always busy. We're going to be busy this year, I must say.

Now tell us, how do you actually do it? What's involved?
It depends a bit on what we're being asked to do, by the client.

Who are your clients? You must get a lot of work from businesspeople.
We do. We get work from everywhere.

And you can extrapolate from quite a small sample, can't you?
We can what from it?

Extrapolate. Once you've built a reliable statistical model, you can assume that on a bigger scale the model will hold.
No, we don't extrapolate. We just cover things.

You cover things?
We cover stuff up, pad it out a bit if necessary, make it look reasonable and make it so you can sit on it properly.

What do you cover up?
Whatever it is, we'll cover it.

I was told you were a polster.
We upholster stuff, yes. Excuse me. Hello Acme Furnishings, Dave speaking.

You're an upholsterer?
Yes. Acme Furnishings. Excuse me. Hello, Dave here. Yes, madam. Yes, we can do that. Where is it? No, I'll bring some samples. What is it exactly? A poll. What sort of poll. A national poll. (Barry we'll need the truck.) Yes, we can freshen it up for you. Give it a bit of life. They can get a bit tired can't they? We'll fix that. How's Tuesday? Where are you? Lodge? Yes, you're a mason, madam. Oh, I see.

Thanks for your time, Dave.
Good on you, Bryan. Will there be someone at home on Tuesday. Tim? Good.

An upholsterer?
No. Sorry, we don't do lawns. We just do upholstering.

Kevin the Second

27 June 2013 – 18 September 2013

Can you perhaps start by telling us what you do?
You work with the government?
I run the government.

OK. And you were involved in an incident.
Tell us what happened.
I was in the Garden of Gethsemane. I was
approached by a group of mongrels including
Mr Iscariot. He and the Pharisees announced
that they were appointing a new leader.

And you were in the wilderness?
Yes.

What happened when you were in the wilderness?
I wrestled with my soul.

And then what happened?
I rose again.

A Cycling Commentator

René and someone else.

Hello in France.
Hello there from Gaul, Bryan.

The tour is at an exciting stage, isn't it?
It is. It's been a great tour so far.

Great interest for Australians this year, of course.
Yes, the Aussies went so well in that first week.

Although the yellow jersey's gone, hasn't it?
Yes, but there are all these other categories, which is what makes the
tour such a great race.

Where are you now?
Western France. Very interesting part of France. Tonight and
tomorrow night we're going through a very old area, a lot of history
around here. Leonardo da Vinci used to live around here, René
Descartes used to live around here.

Who was René Descartes?
He was a famous duellist.

Fought a lot of duels?
Yes, obviously pretty handy in that area.

He must have been good to have survived so many of them.
Yes, I think they both were.

Both who?
I think there were two of them.

Two Descartes?
Yes, René and someone else.

The Descartes brothers?
Yes.

How are the individual Australians going?
A lot of them have dropped out. We've lost Gillard, Swan, Conroy, Emerson, Combet, Smith, Garrett.

So who's left?
Well, we've got Rudd, Albanese, Wong.

There was some controversy with Rudd, wasn't there?
Yes, there was an incident earlier on. There was a bunch sprint and someone went down.

And there were a lot of elbows?
No, there's only one Albo.

He'd go OK in the mountains, wouldn't he?
Albo? He does.

Is Abbott still there?
He is but he's way off the pace.

We see him training a lot here.
That's right, but it's such a tactical race. They've taken the legs out of him up here.

Can he get back on, do you think?
I think he thought if he just sat in the peleton and everyone up the road blew up, he'd be OK.

Hasn't happened?
It never does happen.

So how much time has he lost?
He's now a week and half behind Rudd.

And Rudd's still burning the joint up, isn't he?
Rudd's in the form of his life.

It's a great event and we'll talk to you when they get to Paris.
Yes. Pardon?

What's that?
Apparently Descartes only thought there were two of them. How could he think there were two of them?

The Hon. Bill Shorten
Minister for Education

I'm the member for Maribyrnong.

Bill Shorten, thanks for your time tonight.
Pleasure.

There's been a lot said and written about recent leadership changes in the government.
Yes, the circumstances of the recent changes have been pretty unusual.

Serving prime ministers are not often knifed in office.
I meant that in a couple of recent instances the government's agenda, an important agenda, had been hijacked by speculation about the leadership.

And you had to stop that?
It was damaging the government.

Yes. And there are going to be some changes to the way things are done in that area?
Those changes are to do with ensuring stability, yes.

And now the polls have turned around. It's a different race now, isn't it?
The environment's changed completely.

And you're standing again as the member for Iscariot?
Maribyrnong. I'm the member for Maribyrnong.

Maribyrnong, yes. Out near the Mount of Olives.
Avondale Heights I think you're referring to.

Avondale Heights, yes.
And I'll be offering myself as a candidate in my electorate.

Do you think the poll bounce you've been enjoying will sustain?
It seems very strong in areas where we were in some trouble.

Queensland?
Queensland and New South Wales, yes.

And you and Kevin are getting on well together?
Yes, and Kevin's hit the ground running.

I don't want to go back over the change of leadership, but you gave a press conference before you went into the garden of Gethsemane. What was your thinking there?
I didn't go into the Garden of Gethsemane. I made a brief statement before going into the party room for the vote.

Yes, sorry, *party room* was what I meant to say.
I was going into a meeting with the…

…with the Pharisees?
With the party members and…

…you wanted to make public the decision you'd made?
Yes, I wanted to wear my heart upon my sleeve.

Because you hadn't done that the previous time?
That's right.

Last time you'd been involved in a nasty accident involving a household implement…
…a party discussion involving the leadership of the Australian Labor Party.

Bill Shorten, thanks for your time.
Thank you. *(That's him there. Seize him.)*

The Hon. Kevin Rudd
Prime Minister of Australia

Is there a higher elected official than I am?

Thanks for your time tonight. Are you OK?
Yes, I'm fine.

OK. Now, you were involved in an incident involving safety in the workplace.
I've been involved in a couple of them.

There's another one on Saturday, according to the paper.
Someone wants to have a look at the paper. The paper's part of the problem.

Can you perhaps start by telling us what you do. You work with the government?
I run the government.

You're a government official?
I run the joint.

I'm trying to shield your identity in case what happened to you before happens again.
Is there a higher elected official than I am?

No.
That's right, pal. I'm the bloody government. I'll decide what we change in this interview and we're not changing that. It's changed once and it's not changing again.

OK. And you were involved in an incident. Tell us what happened.
I was betrayed.

You were in fact removed from office, weren't you?
Yes.

And a group of men who were your own people did this to you?
Yes.

Where were you? Tell us what happened.
I was in the Garden of Gethsemane.

That's not where you were, really, is it?
No, I was in my office, in the parliament. You asked me to make up another name for the place.

OK. What happened next?
I was approached by a group of mongrels including Mr Iscariot.

Mr Iscariot was also a member of parliament?
Yes, he's the member for Canaan.

I see. And where is Canaan? It's near the Mount of Olives?
No, it's out near Avondale Heights.

And what did he do?
He and the Pharisees announced that they were appointing a new leader.

And you were in the wilderness?
Yes.

What happened when you were in the wilderness?
I wrestled with my soul.

Some of the disciples were loyal to you, weren't they?
Yes. Some were. They got decent jobs afterwards.

And what happened?
I rose again.

And that's been good for you?
It's a bit early to say.

You seemed happier again, for a while?
Yes, I was, for a while.

Did you sing?
I did, for a while.

What did you sing?
I was all right for a while,
I could smile for a while.

The Abbott Shirtfront

18 September 2013 – 15 September 2015

Your special subject is democracy in Australia. Your questions start now. Who is the current prime minister?
Tony Abbott.

Correct. Who is the preferred prime minister?
Malcolm Turnbull.

Correct. What is Malcolm Turnbull's job?
He's a member of Tony Abbott's government.

Can you give me a bit more detail there?
He's a totally loyal member of Tony Abbott's government.

Correct.

The Hon. Tony Abbott
Prime Minister of Australia

I have to go to a wedding.

Sit up straight, Tony. You know why you're here, don't you?
No. I'm supposed to be going for a bike ride.

You can go for a bike ride later.
I'm supposed to go for a run later.

You can go for a run after you've been for a bike ride.
I can't.

Why not?
I have to go to a wedding.

Tony. You've been made head prefect, Tony. This is a position of considerable responsibility.
Yes, I know.

It's a position you've wanted for a very long time.
Yes.

Now you promised to do certain things once you'd been made head prefect.
Yes. I'll do them. I haven't had time yet.

How are you going with those projects? Let's go through them: the debt crisis, stopping the boats and the carbon tax. Where are you up to with them?
Can I have an extension?

No, you can't. Have you fixed the debt crisis?
Yes.

How have you done that?
We've increased the debt.

You increased the debt?
Yes, we had to.

Why?
I don't know.

You don't know?
No.

Have you asked Joe Hockey?
Yes.

And what did he say?
He doesn't know either.

Have you stopped the boats?
We've introduced a new rule about the boats. It's on the noticeboard.

Is this a new rule that stops boats?
Sort of.

How does it work?
We've made a rule that says you're not allowed to talk about the boats.

Tony, I could stop talking about the weather but that doesn't mean we're not going to have any weather.
It might.

Have you got rid of the carbon tax?
Yes, we're doing that.

And will that reduce electricity prices?
Yes, it will.

No, it won't, Tony. You know very well it won't. We're not even in charge of electricity prices. Electricity prices are made up by people in billing companies.
I've written to them.

Have you got a reply?
Not yet.

When did you write to them?
In 1986.

I understand you've started referring to Shorten as Electricity Bill?
Yes.

Well, that's good. That's much more the sort of leadership we're looking for.
Good.

Have you told him your dad's bigger than his dad?
No, that's good. I'll try that.

Have you told him he's a bandy ape?
That's great.

Just don't tell him you've got half a mind to thrash him.
Why not?

He might agree with you. You've got to be a bit careful.
Words. They're buggers, aren't they?

The Hon. Barnaby Joyce
Minister for Agriculture and Water Resources

A very good wedding.

Barnaby Joyce, thanks for your time.
Pleasure.

You're looking resplendent.
Thanks. Oh this? *(Points to buttonhole.)* I've been to a wedding.

Good wedding? You go to a few weddings, don't you?
I go to as many as I can. I'm a member of the Australian government.

Some members of the government spend a lot of their time at weddings, don't they?
They do. Tony Abbott's the clubhouse leader at the moment but I've got a big weekend coming up.

Was it good? The wedding you've just come from?
This one was a very good wedding.

Well, it's good of you to come into the studio, thanks.
That's fine. I'm sorry I'm a bit late. I got stopped as I was coming out.

You got stopped? Who by?
Some old guy came and started talking to us as we were coming out of the church.

Who's we?
There were three of us. George Brandis and Tony Abbott and myself. This old geezer came and grabbed me by the arm and wouldn't let me go.

Why not?
He wanted to tell me a story.

What was the story?
I'll be writing a full report on this for the finance department, for an expenses claim.

Just briefly?
This guy, as a younger man, had worked on ships, and he had a crossbow and shot a fellow creature.

The old guy? He shot someone?
It was a terrible mistake. The old guy was full of remorse. He wouldn't let go of my arm. 'Unhand me greybeard loon,' I told him.

Had he been drinking?
No. We'd had a couple.

Who did he shoot?
Don't remember all the details. Albert Ross. A bloke called Albert Ross.

Who was Albert Ross?
He must have been a pilot.

A pilot?
Yes, he was flying when he was shot.

Was the old guy arrested?
No, they were at sea. Miles away. But he was punished.

Really? How?
Everything went wrong. It was an omen. The ship stopped, the crew got sick, they got lost, they ran out of water.

Ran out of water? At sea?
Yes, ironical. Water everywhere, as far as the eye can see.

But you can't drink it.
Yes.

Why did everything go wrong?
Because the guy had done the wrong thing.

He'd offended against nature.
Yes. A lot of people, when they do the wrong thing, they go on and on about how it wasn't really wrong or the guidelines are a bit fuzzy or it wasn't their fault. This bloke was full of remorse.

Well, I'm afraid we've run out of time. I must get you back to talk about your portfolio.
I'd better get going.

Where are you going?
I've got to go to the reception.

A Foreign Exchange Trader

Tugga and Gillie and Tubs.

Your name is Nicholas?
Yes.

And what do you do, Nicholas?
I work in the forex room at one of the big banks.

Why would a bank need a baby-food division?
Not farex, forex.

Same age group?
Similar age group. Different name.

I see. And what's your surname, Nicholas?
Name.

Nicholas Name?
Yes.

OK. Your special subject is identifying prominent Australian sporting figures by their full formal titles?
That's right.

Your time starts now. Best of luck.
Thanks.

Correct. Who is Australia's cricket captain?
Pup.

Correct. And who did he take over from?
Punter.

Correct. Who is the coach?
Boof.

Correct. Who was the captain who rebuilt Australian cricket in the 1980s?
Before Tugga and Gillie and Tubs?

Yes.
AB.

Correct. What was Tugga's real name?
Steve Waugh.

Correct. What was the name of his twin brother?
Afghanistan.

Correct. Why?
He was the forgotten Waugh.

Correct. Who is the greatest wicket-taker in Australian cricket history?
Warnie.

Correct. Who won three consecutive Olympic 100-metre freestyle titles?
Dawnie.

Correct. Which tennis player won two grand slams, one as an amateur and one as a professional?
Rocket.

Correct. Who was often said to be the best player never to win Wimbledon?
Muscles.

Correct. Who were the famous doubles pairings who won grand slam titles in the eighties and nineties?
The Maces and the Woodies.

Correct. What was the name of the Belgian who won the Australian Women's Singles title in 2011?
Aussie Kim.

Correct. Who was the Governor of South Australia from 2001 to 2007?
The Lithgow Flash.

Correct. Who's just been dropped as the captain of the Presidents Cup team?
The Shark.

Correct. What is Glenn Lazarus better known as?
Senator the Honorable Brick with Eyes.

Correct. And after that round you've won a book voucher for $13,000.
Great.

Hang on, Nick. Sorry, that's for George Brandis.
George Brandis? I answer the questions and George gets the prize?

Yes, that's the way it works here.
That doesn't seem right.

It does to George, and that's the main thing.
I might have a word with George. I'll be seeing him on Saturday.

Really.
Yes, I go to a lot of weddings. He's often there.

A Police Officer

Stay well away. Report the sighting. Leave the rest to us.

Thanks for your time tonight.
Pleasure.

Now, we're departing this evening from what we would normally do.
That's right and can I thank you for doing this? I realise your time is precious and it's very good of you.

It's a pleasure. This is a pretty important issue.
It is.

Because you're really here to make an appeal to the public, aren't you?
That is correct.

As I understand it, it involves a missing person.
That's right.

Missing since when?
Went missing in December.

That's quite a long time.
It's too long, Bryan.

Is there a description? Can you give us some details?
William Richard Shorten. A male Caucasian.

Age?
Mid to late forties. Two centimetres in height.

That can't be right.
Sorry, 175.2 centimetres.

Where was he last seen?
Last seen in the ACT?

Is that where he lives?
Not certain. He moves about a bit.

Do we know what he was wearing when he was last seen?
A business suit, white shirt, blue tie.

Have you got a picture? It might help if people could see what he looks like. *(Identikit picture comes up.)* **And is this a person of interest?**
Yes, it is and just a note of caution. He should not be approached.

So if people do see this person they should keep away?
Stay well away. Report the sighting. Leave the rest to us.

What he's alleged to have done?
There have been a couple of knifing incidents at his workplace.

Were these workplace accidents?
They may have been, Bryan, but in the case of the second one he went on national television to announce he was about to do it.

Oh dear. And do you think he might have become the victim of a knifing himself?
We don't believe so, no. There have been a couple of reported sightings.

Where?
One in London. One in Paris.

Paris? What was he doing in Paris?
We've got no idea. Obviously we'd like to talk to him about that.

And what alerted you to the fact that he was missing?
He hasn't been at work.

What does he do?
William is believed to be the leader of the parliamentary opposition.

He's the leader of the opposition?
Yes.

I think I've seen him.

Since December?

No, not in the period since he's been missing.

We're very anxious to talk to him. Obviously if he's no longer interested in the job we'd need to get someone else in there very quickly.

Yes. You can't have no opposition.

That's right. But our main concern, Bryan, is for his safety.

Of course. Thanks for your time.

It's very good of you to do this. And thank you.

Two Senior Political Officials

Ours has a white cover.

Thank you both for your time tonight.
1. Pleased to be here.
2. Good to be with you.

We asked for the minister for immigration and the opposition spokesman on immigration.
1. The minister's busy.
2. So is the unminister.

You've both been sent here to answer these questions. You are both senior officials.
1. I'm a senior official with the immigration ministry.
2. I'm here as an opposition spokesman.

OK. Now, the question of how Australia deals with asylum seekers has been in the news lately because of a major disturbance at the Manus Island detention centre, a disturbance in which a man was killed.
2. That's right.
1. Yes.

Let's discuss that briefly. What went wrong there?
1. The government inherited a complete shambles when it came into government and we're doing everything we can to fix it. In some respects we've done very well. This tragic accident is an isolated incident and we're obviously making inquiries into how it happened.
2. The government has been fear-mongering about asylum seekers for years and they've now cranked up the secrecy and the draconian treatment of these people and it's coming apart in their hands.

What are the policy differences between you on this issue?
1. I've got our policy here. We can go through it.
2. I've got our policy here.

OK. So what are we going to do? These people are in a jail set up by Australia.

1. They're not prisoners.

Isn't the place they're in a jail?

2. It is but they're not prisoners. They're asylum seekers.

1. They're only in jail while they're being processed.

And how long does that take?

1. I'll get that for you 'as soon as possible'.

2. Yes. 'As soon as possible.'

We clearly have a problem with immigration policy. What are the differences between the policies of the two major parties?

1. Ours has a white cover.

2. White cover on ours too.

1. Need to process asylum seekers offshore.

2. There's a semicolon. We've just got a comma there.

1. That's just a mark on the page.

2. OK.

Why don't we process asylum seekers in Australia? This must be costing us a fortune.

2. Hang on. We're looking for the differences. Let's find the differences. What's that?

1. That's the definition for 'as soon as possible'.

2. Same as ours.

We might leave it there. Thanks for your time tonight.

1. Thanks, Bryan. List of foreign contractors.

2. Acme Surveillance to Zenith Fencing.

1. Yes, that's the same.

2. Is that a footnote?

1. Yes.

2. What does it say?

1. I'm afraid I can't tell what it says.

2. Same as ours.

1. Cricket was good, wasn't it?

2. Great match. Great series.

Mr Glenn Stevens
Governor of the Reserve Bank
of Australia

Perhaps if all the children join hands.

Glenn Stevens, thanks for joining us.
It's a very significant pleasure to be here.

Thank you.
If there's a greater pleasure, Bryan, than engaging with you in a discussion of economics whatever you perceive that to be, it certainly isn't something of which I'm currently aware.

I'm also overjoyed, if it's any comfort.
Power is often exercised in its restraint, Bryan. How can I help you?

The Reserve Bank has made its monthly decision about interest rates.
I'm probably supposed to say something here, am I?

And you left interest rates unchanged.
We did.

As you did last month, too.
Indeed.

And you issued a statement.
That's right. That's one of the KPIs in our area.

It, too, was the same as the previous month's.
Yes, Bryan. We're not trying to attract attention. We're trying to run an important aspect of the economy.

Have you got an app for doing this, have you?
An app. What's an app?

An application.
I was seeking information there about the meaning of the expression.

An application is a type of technology designed for telephony.
Perhaps if all the children join hands.

What I mean is the system is very predictable.
A lot of people have a gift for predicting the past, Bryan. It's
surprisingly common in your line of work, for example.

Maybe you're not aware of how obvious it is, what you're going to do.
We get a lot of this, Bryan. We get this all the time.

I'm not surprised you get a bit of this. Who do you get it from?
Other Nobel laureates mostly. How would an app work?

Well, if you put rates up a bell would ring.
A bell. We might struggle with our excitement levels down at the RBA.

The bell would indicate a rise in the currency.
And what would we do?

You'd lower interest rates back down?
And then what would happen?

You'd get a kind of swanee-whistle sound.
And what would that be?

That would be house prices going up.
And so what would we do then?

You'd put interest rates back where they were.
What would happen if you altered the marginal spending propensities
in the Chinese domestic economy?

**We wouldn't have a button for that. This is about the Australian
economy.**
I see. Would it have a button for politely excusing yourself from an
interview?

Well, I'm sure you could devise an app that would have all the right variables in it.
I hope you're right, Bryan.

It would put you out of a job, of course.
I don't know about that. The people designing this crap.

App.
App, my apologies. The people designing this app might need some assistance.

What sort of thing, do you think?
More crayons. Some fairy bread.

A lot of these people would be financial advisors.
I don't think there's any doubt about that, Bryan.

Thanks for your time.
Be still my beating heart.

Nick, A Quiz Show Contestant

I don't recall.

Your name is Nick.
Yes, that's right.

And what's your surname, Nick.
de Silva.

OK, Nick. And your special subject tonight is Arthur Sinodinos.
No. Hang on. Can I correct you there? That's not right.

Says here your special subject is Arthur Sinodinos.
I'm not aware that that's the case.

You're not aware that your special subject is Arthur Sinodinos?
That's right.

Were you aware that you had a special subject?
Yes, that was my understanding.

How did you think it was selected?
I don't recall exactly how the subject was selected.

Wouldn't you have chosen your own special subject?
As I say, I don't remember exactly how it was done.

Do you accept that it is your subject?
My subject is my subject. I'm just not sure this is it.

Nick, if you didn't select your subject, who do you think did?
I'm not aware of the process whereby the subject was chosen.

If the subject was chosen by someone else, you must have been told what it was at some point. Do you accept that?
I don't recall being informed about it, no.

So you didn't select the subject listed here as your special subject?
I didn't.

And you don't recall having been informed about it?
That's right.

So how do you think it happened?
As I've already said, I was unaware that it had happened.

Do you know anything about Arthur Sinodinos?
Nothing at all.

Have you ever met Arthur?
Not that I recall.

Do you know who he is?
No. It's not a name I recognise.

Are you aware there is a person called Arthur Sinodinos?
I am aware of that because you're asking me about him but I wasn't previously aware that he was involved in any of this in any way at all.

Is this your handwriting?
Yes.

Can you read me what that says there?
Arthur Sinodinos.

I'll ask you again. Who is Arthur Sinodinos?
I've got no idea.

You wrote that Nick. And you're telling me you don't know who he is?
That's right.

No further questions, Nick. You haven't really answered at all. Well done.
Yes!

Stan, A Quiz Show Contestant

A complete treasurer.

Your name is Stan.
That's right.

And what line of work are you in Stan?
It's hard to explain.

Give it a go, Stan.
I'd rather not say exactly what I do.

Can you give us some idea?
I'm a scientist.

You're a scientist?
Yes.

That must be interesting. And what do you do for a living, Stan.
That's what I do. I'm a scientist.

That's what you do for living?
Yes.

In Australia?
Yes.

Well, good for you. Follow your dream. Have you got a surname, Stan?
Dingup.

Stan Dingup?
That's right.

OK, Stan. Your special subject tonight is Australian usage?
Yes. Of the English language.

That's right. The way we use the English language in Australia.
That's right.

Which is sometimes rather distinctive.
We do have our own way of saying things.

Your questions start now. Good luck.
Thanks.

What is it called when you say something you know to be false?
A policy?

Not quite.
Is it a reform? An important reform. A much-needed reform. Long overdue.

No, Stan, it's a lie. If you promised you were going to do something and then you did the opposite, what would you be...
...prime minister?

No, you'd be a complete...
...treasurer? A complete treasurer?

No, you'd be a complete liar, Stan. If you add to the cost of something by charging an impost which goes to the government, what is that called?
Nation-building?

What is the actual amount called?
A levy?

No. I'll give you a clue, Stan. It goes to the tax office.
A gift?

No, it's not a gift Stan. It's compulsory.
Is it a co-payment?

No, it's a tax.
Hang on. You're saying these answers are all just standard English usage?

Stan, the questions are about the use of English in Australia.

Yes, but the answers are all about the actual meaning of the words.

That's correct.

I thought the way the words worked in Australia was different.

A lot of people thought that Stan, but it's not true.

It's a lie.

Yes, I'm sorry, you haven't done very well here.

That's all right. I'm delighted that words have an actual meaning.

It's a relief, isn't it?

Yes. Thank God for that.

The Hon. Scott Morrison
Minister for Immigration and
Border Protection

You won't be asking any questions?

Scott Morrison, thanks for your time tonight.
Pleasure to be with you. Very good to be here. What would you like to talk about?

I'm not going to tell you.
This'll be interesting. You're not going to tell me what it is you'd like to discuss?

No.
I won't be able to answer your questions if you don't tell me what they are.

No, I won't be asking any questions.
You won't be asking any questions?

No.
Isn't that why you're here? To ask questions. Isn't that what you do?

I'm here to help provide information to the public about the issues outlined for discussion.
You're telling me you're not going to do that.

That's what I'm telling you.
You're actually refusing to do what you've just defined as your job?

I am doing my job.
No, you're not. You've just said you're not going to do it.

Why do you think I'm here?
I don't know why you're here. Why would you just turn up and announce that this is your job and you're not going to do it?

I'm not saying that. I'm describing how I'm going to do it.
By not doing it.

It's my job. I'll decide how to do it.
It's never been done like that before.

Maybe that's part of the problem.
Let me put something to you. Bryan, I'm the immigration minister.
I have a number of areas of responsibility and there are some very
important things to say. It's imperative that we get some of these very
important messages out there.

You're entitled to your view. I respect that. Thanks for coming in.
Bryan. I want to talk to you. You've got a national audience. We need
to get some messages out there.

There's a noticeboard in the foyer.
We need to send a message out to people-smugglers.

**Well, go and talk to them. Why come in here if you want to get a
message to people-smugglers?**
You're being impossible!

As a matter of interest I learnt this attitude to my work from you.
From me?

**Yes. You don't tell anyone what's going on. You don't answer
questions. I agree with you. Why bother? I won't ask them.**
I do answer questions.

**No, you don't. You flannel about, you lose your temper, you say things
that don't make sense and then you leave.**
The government has a policy of not talking about operational matters.

The government doesn't talk about anything else.
We only discuss operational matters in order to point out that we're not
going to discuss them.

Have a look at the paper. It's all operational matters and sport.
Ask me anything.

Why?
Yes, sorry. Can we have an easier one to start with?

Phillip, A Quiz Show Contestant

A framework for the recognition of achievement.

Your name is the Sir Prince Duke?
No, my name is Phillip.

Yes, sorry, I'm in a Gilbert and Sullivan production. I'm reading from one of the songs. And what's your surname, Phillip?
McCavity.

And what line of work are you in, Phil?
I'm a dentist.

And you've got a very interesting special subject here. The Australian honours system. Has that always interested you?
Yes, I think I got interested as a kid and I've always followed it quite closely.

Good for you. Have you ever received one?
An honour?

Yes.
No. No, I haven't.

Well, here's hoping. Your questions start now, Phil. What is the Australian honours system?
It is a framework for the recognition of achievement in various fields by Australians.

I'm afraid we can't accept that.
It is a system for honouring significant achievements by Australians.

No, I'm sorry.
It's a system for the recognition of contributions made to Australian life, in various fields, sport, public life, in defence, in business…

No. You're getting further away here, Phil. I'll just repeat the question. What is the Australian honours system?

I know this. It's a system for acknowledging significant contributions to the public life of Australia by its citizens, famous ones sometimes like Bradman, sometimes lesser known ones, but people who have helped other people.

I don't know what you're talking about there, Phil, but I'm afraid I can only go with what's written here. I'll give you one more crack at this. What is the Australian honours system?

It's a system that announces public honours conferred on Australians.

No. We'll move on, I think. What is *The Lion King*?

Can I ask what the answer was to the previous question?

Stop the clock for a second, Shane. The question was 'What is the Australian honours system?' The answer we were looking for was 'A children's fantasy'.

Hang on. That's the answer to the next question.

No, it's not. The next question is 'What is *The Lion King*?'

Yes, a children's fantasy.

No, *The Lion King* is a musical based partly on *Hamlet*.

But it's a children fantasy.

OK. Next question. What is *The Lion King*?

It's a children's fantasy.

That is incorrect. It is a person who has lost touch with reality. What is a lunatic?

I'm not answering any more of these, Bryan. I know what I'm doing.

Correct. Who is Tony Abbott?

No, I'm gone, Bryan.

You're going nicely now, Phil.

Yes, I'm getting the hang of it now.

Leslie, A Quiz Show Contestant

How can an answer be a question?

Your name is Leslie.
That's right.

And what do you do, Leslie?
I work in hospitality.

Really. And what does that involve?
There's a pub not far from where I live.

And you go there a bit, do you?
Yes, I've been going there for some time.

OK. And what's your surname, Les?
Miserables.

Righto, Les. Your special subject is answering every question with a question.
That's my what?

That's your special subject.
What is?

Answering every question with a question.
Really?

That's what it says here.
Answering every question with a question?

Yes.
How can an answer be a question? Isn't a question the opposite of an answer?

That's nevertheless what you're apparently going to attempt.
Is that right?

Yes. Here we go. What is the purpose of the federal government?
In Australia?

Yes.
The current government?

Any government.
How many federal governments have we got?

We've got one federal government and one federal opposition.
We've got a federal opposition?

Yes.
Are you sure?

Yes, they're trying to get a gay marriage bill into the parliament.
Gay marriage is illegal?

Yes, it's not legal in Australia.
Why isn't gay marriage legal?

A lot of people think the purpose of marriage is to have children.
Who says gay people can't have children?

Of course they can and a great many do.
Do I look surprised?

Pardon?
Am I bothered?

Pardon?
Am I bothered?

What I mean is a lot of gay people are married.
Didn't you just say that was illegal?

It's not illegal for them to be married. It's illegal for them to be married to each other.
So who are they married to now?

A lot of them aren't married at all. They're not allowed to be.
But they can have children?

They can.
Which is the alleged purpose of marriage?

Some people believe that, yes.
So you can cook a meal but only if you don't have a kitchen.

I'm afraid that wasn't a question, Les.
It's certainly not an answer.

You've done pretty well, anyway. You've won the presidency of FIFA.
OK. Great. Do I get a bucket?

A bucket?
Yes, what am I going to put it in?

Copernicus, A Quiz Show Contestant

An irrational tetrahedron.

Your name is Copper Knickers.
No. My name is Copernicus.

Copernicus. I beg your pardon.
Copernicus Jackson.

I beg your pardon.
That's OK.

And what sort of work do you do?
I'm an actuary.

What is an actuary?
We calculate risk, in the insurance industry, so insurers can be covered
in terms of their exposure, and reinsurance.

And in fact your special subject is mathematics?
Yes.

**Good luck. Your questions start now. If you're dividing eighteen by
six, what is the quotient?**
Three.

Correct. How many prime numbers are there ending with four?
None.

Correct. What do the angles inside a triangle add up to?
One hundred and eighty degrees.

**Correct. Beethoven proposed marriage to Josephine Brunsvik on
several occasions. What was her response each time?**
Nine.

Correct. How many World Drivers' Championships did the Argentinian driver Fangio win?
Five.

Correct. What was Fangio's first name?
One.

Correct. How many previous leaders of his party has the prime minister ousted?
Two.

Correct. What does Turnbull's Law state?
For every action there is an equal and opposite perfectly reasonable-sounding explanation with quite a lot of hand movements.

Correct. What is Barnaby Joyce?
A perfect square. No, hang on, he might be an irrational tetrahedron.

No, he's the member for New England. What is a Mandelbrot set?
When Mandelbrot gets his serve and volley game working and….

Are you talking about tennis?
Yes.

Why?
Just a random idea.

Correct. Joe Hockey liked to smoke cigars but what did he have for lunch?
Twenty-two over seven. With sauce.

Correct. What is the mathematical term for Bill Shorten?
A set with no members.

Correct. What's the difference between Euclidean and non-Euclidean geometry?
Euclid.

Yes, but what is the principle which is in one but not in the other?
The parallel postulate.

Correct. If you were looking at an Australian politician from the back of a hall…
Was I higher up?

Yes. You were above the politician; how would you describe your perspective of the politician?
Was the politician talking?

Yes.
The angle of depression.

Correct. Superb round. A perfect score.
Great.

And you have won a fifty per cent increase in the GST.
I don't know that I like the sound of that.

It'll happen in bits. You'll hardly notice.
As long as there's some sport.

A Cricket Commentator

What a knock.

Welcome back, and let's bring you up to date with what's been happening here where Menzies won the toss in ideal conditions and elected to bat on what looked like a pretty good wicket.
And they were helped by some pretty ordinary bowling in that first session.

They were.
Brilliant 126 from Menzies himself. He played beautifully.

Quite good support from Holt, who unfortunately threw his wicket away.
Shouldn't have gone out.

No, he was on thirty-five and they might regret that. We then saw a sparkling century from Gorton before he was run out.
Now that was interesting. It looked like Fraser's call from up here.

It did, but we're on a bit of an angle but there was certainly some confusion. It took the bowlers a while to get rid of Fraser.
It wasn't until they brought Hawke on that he looked in any trouble at all really.

A very good spell from Hawke. He troubled all the batsmen.
He did. Howard was there for two hours for seven. The tail didn't wag much and they were all out for 377.

So the ALP needed 378 for victory, and what a story this has been. We saw Calwell and Whitlam come out to open. First ball Gorton got one to nip back and Calwell was out without playing a shot.
Whitlam. What a knock.

Yes. A famous knock, I would think.
It was magnificent.

He took what looked like a pretty good attack and he carted them all over the ground.
Took the bowling apart.

He scored his first fifty off sixteen deliveries. He got a hundred from forty-one deliveries. They didn't know what do.
Controversial dismissal.

He was out under very controversial circumstances. He was looking to sweep down leg side, Fraser caught the ball and the slips all went up.
There was nothing on snicko.

I don't think it hit the pads and he was given out. They went upstairs.
They've got to stop doing this.

They went upstairs. Umpire Kerr called for drinks and Whitlam was given out. Then we saw Hawke come in and completely dominate for a marvellous ninety-four.
Great support from Keating.

Great support from Keating, who got seventy-eight.
And then the collapse.

Yes, we saw Beazley go out to a terrible shot.
No feet.

No suggestion of footwork whatever. Crean out first ball. Latham skittled by the very next ball. Didn't offer a shot.
Howard on a hat-trick.

That's right. Rudd made thirty-six, was run out, was then recalled, made two more and was out to a very good ball from Shorten.
Wasn't it Abbott?

No, if you have a look at the replay it comes off Shorten. So we've got Gillard out there on twenty-six and chasing 377, the ALP are 372 for nine. Shorten is coming to the wicket and Turnbull's decided to have a bowl himself.

This will be interesting. How many do they need?

They need six runs from this final over.

What's Abbott doing?

What is Abbott doing? He's stamping on the ball. Oh, this is childish.

He won't give Turnbull the ball. Oh, this is unfortunate.

What a shame. We might have a bit of a delay here. What'll we do, Bryan?

There's a seagull down at deep fine leg.

So there is. What's he eating?

A chip.

The Turnbull Restoration

15 September 2015 –

Malcolm Turnbull, thanks for your time.
Good to be with you, Bryan.

Now, the parliament's back.
It is, Bryan, and we've got a great opportunity here.
As a nation. We can achieve great things here.

You've got a majority of one.
Try not to interrupt, Bryan.

The Hon. Malcolm Turnbull
Prime Minister of Australia

And let me say this.

Malcolm Turnbull, thanks for your time.
Pleasure.

How are you? Are you enjoying playing a slightly bigger role now, as prime minister?
Well, I am and, Bryan, if I can just go to your earlier question first.

Earlier question?
Yes, you asked how I am. I'll take them in order.

You mean 'How are you?'
Yes. I'm very busy but I'm enjoying it enormously. We face great challenges, Bryan. I think what we need to do is to confront these challenges and to flush from them the opportunities contained within them. And let me say this: whatever the future holds, we'll do well to approach it with openness and with intelligence. Hiding in the dark isn't an option.

Yes but...
...more importantly, to continue with my response to your (in my view perhaps even slightly better) second question, I think there's a feeling in the broader Australian public that there is greater agility in government and greater momentum now. When I move among the people, ordinary people, people like me and you...

There is a great deal of destabilising going on too, though, isn't there?
I don't want to make too much of that.

But there are leaks coming out every day. There's a real attempt to undermine…

…if there are those who are unhappy about the restoration, their intriguing will either wither on the vine…

…or they'll take you out in a box.

Well. You might be right. That's the system. But to go back to what I said a minute ago, thirty seconds ago, forty seconds ago, there are going to be challenges. Let's be invigorated by them.

OK. You've made several changes. Obviously we have a new treasurer. You're trying to address public outrage about what's going on in detention camps. We have a completely new rhetoric on the cultural diversity within Australia.

We must work together…

We have a new arts minister.

That's right.

Are these areas where you thought the government was failing?

Not in every case, Bryan. Let's take them one at a time.

Let's do the arts ministry first because George Brandis's idea of excellence didn't prove to be a beacon for a lot of artists.

OK.

I've written a book.

Have you? Submit it to the new arts minister, whose name is *(Reads.)* Reward Mitchell. Go and see Reward.

No, it's Mitch Fifield.

Go and see him. What sort of book is it?

A children's book. I'll read you a bit.

Go ahead.

'With one bound Malcolm was free.'

Free from what?

It doesn't say.

Free of the past maybe. I do hope so. It's a great concept.

"'We're starting again," said Malcolm. "Follow me." And he set off down the road to the future. Some followed him. But others didn't.' The smart ones probably did. That sounds great. Go and see Reward. He'll love it.

How do you know he'll love it?

A Shopping Channel Host

The gift-giving season.

OK. Now you have some products to show us.
I do. Am in the right position? Is this OK?

Yes, you're fine.
I'm normally standing up, on the other channels. It's easier to get excited when you're standing up.

No, this is good. This is what the ABC has needed for a long time. Can you just keep the products down a bit.
You're not going to show the products?

No. We don't do that here. You can talk about them, but you can't show them.
OK. We've got the gift-giving season coming up. Do you like reading, Bryan?

I love reading.
Tony Abbott's history.

I think we all saw that coming.
No, I mean he's written a history book.

Really. What's it called?
It's called *The Future for Australia*. It's not actually one of our better performing units. Here you go. With so many people living in apartments in the city, without a garden, this sits on your table or your bench.

What a gorgeous little plant. What is it?
This is a Christopher pine.

What does it do?
It blows in the wind. Watch this. If there's any breeze, even the slightest little breeze…

…it's moving now…

…it is, the slightest movement of the air and there it is, up and busy.

I could look at that all day.

It'd love that. Now look at this. Kids will love this.

Oh, that's a Bernardi!

That's right.

I've read about these. They're great.

They are.

What do they do?

This top part comes off, you fill it with water, plug it in and after a minute steam comes out the ears and listen to this. *(Yapping sound.)*

It barks.

It barks and the arms wave around.

How do you stop it?

Turn this switch off. Now, a lot of people are very difficult to buy for. Here's something that gets around that. You can give this one to anyone because it's actually for the house.

Great idea.

Here you go. It's a Malcolm spray, comes in a range of sizes and two different applicators.

What's a Malcolm spray?

Well, if your house smells a bit of politics…

…which they all do…

…yes, who isn't familiar with that one, you just give a couple of squirts with the Malcolm spray.

Gone.

No one would know any politics had ever been there. You've got guests coming over for that important dinner. There's still a bit of politics hanging around…

...you squirt the Malcolm spray.
You don't need a lot, Bryan.

Nice smell.
You can get it in a few fragrances. This one's 'waffle'.

Fantastic.
We've got a special offer on these at the moment. How many would you like?

We don't do offers on the ABC.
I'll leave them in the foyer. People can come and get them.

Thanks for bringing them in and have a great Christmas.
If you buy some of these, Bryan, I'll have a ripper.

A Social Researcher

A bellwether electorate.

Thanks for your time tonight.
Good to be here.

Your company conducts social research.
That's right.

Can I take you to this poll you released this week into voting intentions?
Yes.

How is this sort of research done?
We do it by phone, mobile phones, we talk to people in the street, we look at social media.

Do you do it all over the country?
We try to.

Let's go through key electorates. Let's have a look at Faffing.
Faffing, good example. This is a bellwether electorate.

Faffing's quite a big electorate.
Faffing's huge. It's one of the biggest electorates in the country.

It takes in Drivel, doesn't it?
It takes in everything from Drivel up through Flannel, Promise and out to Dissemble up to Mount Excuses.

The Empty runs down through there.
The Empty runs down through Promise, yes.

So where does it start?
The Empty? Starts further up. In the adjoining electorate. In Wallop.

Is it true that there's a big swing on in Wallop?

That's what we're hearing. Wallop has been held for a long time by the National Party and, look, it's a bit difficult to tell what's going on up there.

Why?

They haven't got the NBN so you can only talk to them if there's a full moon and a light westerly.

But are they happy with the services they've got up there?

In Wallop?

Yes.

No, the services are down here in Faffing.

Schools, hospitals and so on.

There's a new school planned for Promise. There's quite a good hospital in Flannel.

So they're happy?

They haven't got a doctor but the carpark's nice.

What about the city electorates? Let's have a look at Plutocrat. There's been a redistribution there, hasn't there?

No. I don't think there's ever been a redistribution in Pluto.

I thought some of it had gone to Trading.

That's the state seat.

Where are Scoundrel and Entitlement?

They're both inside Trading. Federally Pluto takes them in but also takes in Drinkies, Upper Drinkies, One More and Ireallymustgo.

What's the river that goes through there?

The Onan.

Beautiful.

Lovely area right through there.

Is the Great Barrier Reef an electorate?
It used to be. The Great Barrier Reef is now in the electorate of
Coalmine.

And who's the sitting member?
India.

India? That can't be right.
'India, c/- Greg Hunt.'

The electoral commission might need to look at that.
Yes.

Who's Greg Hunt?
I don't know but somebody must have voted for him or he wouldn't
be there.

A Political Commentator

A failure of leadership.

Thanks for your time tonight.
Good to be with you.

I'd like to talk about Brexit. This is a big thing for Britain, isn't it?
This is huge. It's decisive. This will not only affect the way the British economy works. This will affect the social development of Britain as a nation.

Can you explain how the current situation developed?
Yes. In a nutshell, it's a failure of leadership. The prime minister had a particular view, a particular set of policies, not everyone in his own party agreed with him…

This is in Britain?
Yes. There were right-wing elements in his own party, and there were opportunists who would seize on any weakness, and he was under a huge amount of internal pressure. A lot of this was leaked to the press. He was being sabotaged…

You're talking about events in Britain?
Yes. The prime minister had come from a particular background, he was wealthy, he had been mentioned in some distant context in relation to the Panama Papers.

This is the British prime minister?
Yes, and there was a view, a widespread view, that the prime minister was completely out of touch with the ordinary people…

Hang on, I'm not asking about Australian politics. I'm asking you about this recent vote in Britain.
That's what I'm talking about. The prime minister got it wrong. The whole business of getting people to vote was a colossal mistake. He thought that if he went to the people he would carry the day, defeat the

opposition, get rid of the people in his own party who were trying to get rid of him…

Look, can I just stop you there? I've got you on here to talk about the situation in Britain.
Yes.

You're supposed to be an expert on what's just happened in Britain.
Yes.

Well, can you just confine yourself to talking about Britain? I don't want to know about Australia. I know what's just happened in Australia. I live in Australia.
Right. The prime minister went to the people and he took an absolute towelling. He was in a worse position *after* the vote than he was before it. And then there's the Scot problem.

The Scott problem?
Yes.

The Scott problem in Britain?
How are they going to fix that? It's been festering for a while, that one.

This is hopeless. How's the weather?
Today? Wet and cold. It was raining earlier.

I don't want to know what's happening here. I mean in Britain.
I'm taking about Britain.

What's the future for the British economy, do you think?
We're facing some serious issues. Debt is a big issue here. The gap between the rich and the poor is widening and this is what I was talking about earlier. A lot of people thought the prime minister was out of touch. That's one of the reasons we got the result we got.

I give up. I'm asking about Britain!

Senator Sam Dastyari
Former Manager of Opposition Business in the Senate

It was an error of judgment.

Senator Dastyari, thanks for your time.
Thank you, Bryan. Can I just repeat something I said earlier?

You haven't said anything earlier.
No, but let me just repeat it. It's important. I don't want there to be any misunderstanding about this. I want this message.to get through.

You can't repeat something you haven't already said.
I can't if you won't let me.

Hang on, Senator Dastyari. I haven't asked you anything yet.
But, just before you do, let me repeat what I've already said…

Senator Dastyari, you can't repeat something you haven't already said.
If you just allow me to make a brief statement it will contain the elements I want to repeat.

I don't know what you're talking about.
Bryan, we have a great deal in common. I'm just like you. I'm human. And, look, I made a mistake. I did something I shouldn't have done. It was an error of judgment. I'm not trying to pretend it didn't happen. It did happen. I want to take responsibility for it. It was my fault.

Can I ask you a question?
Anything.

Why did you ask someone associated with the government of a foreign country to pay your travel expenses?

That is a very pertinent question. I agree with your question. That's exactly the question I'd ask if I were in your position. Why would a person do that? Is there influence being bought? Was the money actually sought, and if so under what terms and conditions?

What's the answer?

That's exactly what I'd want to know. You've put your finger on it. You could circle this sort of thing all day and get distracted from the real issue. There's really only one question and you've put your finger on it.

What's the answer?

Let me say this. I made a mistake. I did something I shouldn't have done. It was an error of judgment. I'm not trying to pretend it didn't happen. It did. I want to take responsibility for it. It was my fault.

Why did you ask for money from this particular source?

Bryan. Listen to what I'm saying. I made an error of judgment. I want to take responsibility for it. It was my fault.

Why did you do it?

It was a mistake. I'm to blame for this whole thing. I got it wrong.

What's the capital of Norway?

I made a mistake. I did something I shouldn't have done. It was an error of judgment. I'm not trying to pretend it didn't happen. It did. I want to take responsibility for it. It was my fault.

Senator Dastyari, thanks for your time.

I was wrong. I made a mistake.

Thanks for your time.

Have we finished?

I think we probably need to wait and see.

Bugger it.

Are you being picked up?
No.

Why not?
I did something I shouldn't have done. It was an error of judgment.
I'm not trying to pretend it didn't happen. It did. I want to take
responsibility for it. It was my fault.

Senator George Brandis
Attorney-General of Australia

We promised, if elected, to bring in a plebiscite.

George Brandis, thanks for your time.
My pleasure to be here, Bryan.

This plebiscite you're organising. We don't have a lot of these, do we?
No, we don't, Bryan. A plebiscite is just a device provided for in the Australian constitution, used principally in cases where it is considered a good idea to go and ask the public what they think.

Haven't the people just expressed their view in the recent election?
In the recent election, Bryan, an election I might say that the government won resoundingly…

By one seat.
It won it resoundingly, Bryan. We won that election. We've got a majority. You speak to Christopher Pyne. We won that election. We promised, if elected, to bring in a plebiscite.

But we don't have a plebiscite on all issues that are considered important, do we?
No, we don't. Not on all issues. But on significant social issues we do have the capacity to go to the people and say 'People, what do you think?' A lot of countries don't have this. The Labor Party doesn't want you to have it. They want to strip your democratic rights away, Bryan, that what's they want to do.

Let's not talk about the Labor Party. George Brandis, why does same-sex marriage require a change to the Marriage Act?
Because the Marriage Act was amended in 2004 specifically in order to preclude this possibility. Marriage has to be between a man and a woman currently.

Why did the Australian public want that change made?
They didn't want it. The government just brought that in.

The government just did it?
Yes, the government just did it.

So sometimes the government actually does things? Is that right?
Governments do things all the time. We're doing things.

What is this government doing at the moment?
We're organising a plebiscite into same-sex marriage, Bryan.
That's why I'm here talking to you.

This doesn't make sense. The Australian public was opposed, for example, to the bombing of Iraq. Why wasn't a plebiscite held over that?
I think the thought there, Bryan, was that the Australian people's opposition to bombing Iraq was not an idea that yearned for expression.

Although we did have a public vote on whether or not to become a republic.
We did, famously so, yes.

With what result?
That proposed change was defeated.

I thought people wanted a republic.
They did. I think the thought there is that the wrong question was asked.

That's clever.
That was very, very clever.

So the case for the republic had the support of the Australian public and was defeated in the vote?
Yes.

Who was running the case for a republic?

I just forget his name, Bryan, but that's certainly not going to happen again.

Why not?

Because we've got our foot to the floor on this. We've got all the stops on this organ pulled right out. We'll carry the day here, don't you worry about that.

George Brandis, how's the government going?

It's going well. We won a trophy this week.

A trophy? What was it?

I don't know what it was for. I just saw the headline. I didn't read the story. Here it is.

Can I see it?

Yes. 'AUSTRALIAN GOVERNMENT A TROPHY.'

'AUSTRALIAN GOVERNMENT ATROPHY.'

I beg your pardon?

'Australian government atrophy.'

No, it's not atrophy. There's supposed to be a gap between the A and the T. Atrophy? Why would anybody say that?

George Brandis, thanks for your time.

I'll ring that media outlet, Bryan. That's the third time they've done that.

The Hon. Malcolm Turnbull
Prime Minister of Australia

It's just a crossword.

Prime minister, we'll start in a minute. We've got some sort of camera problem.
OK. Fine.

What I'd like to do is go through these recent poll figures which I'm afraid aren't terribly good.
God, these things are hard, aren't they?

What is it?
It's just a crossword. I was doing it in the plane. It says it's 'easy'. There's a hard one over here. I'm doing the easy one. I don't know.

(Off.) We'll wait but how long?
'Locality within the city of Vincent, in Perth.'

Any clues?
Six letters. 'Somethingville.'

I don't know Perth very well. Barnettville?
Doesn't fit.

What's that short one?
'Something and the Swan. Greek mythological story.'

How many letters?
Four.

I don't know anything about Greek mythology.
Try this one. Do you know anything about music?

Depends what sort of music.
'German songs from the romantic period.'

German songs?
Yes, from the romantic period.

German songs. Any letters?
Begins with an L.

How do you know that?
Fourteen across is superannuation policy.

Backflip.
Yes, so the L is right.

German songs?
Have a go at this one. 'English city, home to Headingly.'

Headingly. Famous cricket ground.
Yes. Do you know where it is?

Is it in Nottingham?
No. Five letters. Begins with L. Second letter is an E. On the assumption that six down is correct.

What is it?
'Cave in to your own right wing.'

Plebiscite.
Yes, and ten down is 'Runaway train, six letters'.

Budget.
Yes, so it's L E – – –.

What's that one at the top?
Three across. 'Breeches made of leather.'

Is it something to do with Christopher Pyne?
'Something hosen.' I think it starts with L.

Why?
What sort of tick is Malcolm Roberts?

Lunar.

Yes, so something hosen begins with an L.

What's that one there?

I've got that one. 'The act of leading a group or nation.' Ten letters.

What have you written?

'Compromise.'

What about 'leadership'. The act of leading. 'Leadership.' Ten letters.

Oh. Have you got a rubber?

(Off.) You right? We're ready, Prime Minister. We'll start now. Aren't you going to change your answer?

No. I'm pretty sure that's right. I've just got something on my tie. I'd better look the part.

A Political Commentator

Only one candidate who can.

What's going on in the US? The spectacle element seems to have got out of hand.
We've got one debate to go and, yes, it was thought to be a pretty even tussle a few weeks ago, but it's looking increasingly as if...

...democracy might not be the answer...
...there might really be only one candidate who can actually...

...eliminate reason on every issue...
...claim to be fit for the office of president.

The Republican Party is in trouble either way here, isn't it? If they win their hands are tied and if they lose they've got to rebuild a political party.
Yes, the Republicans have had a...

...a hostile takeover...
...rough time. As much as anything, what's happened here is that a...

...a spoilt narcissist...
...a candidate who built a public profile on reality television and can bring a huge...

...respect for women...
...constituency, which is a massive TV audience, to the Republican cause, can't do that without...

...making a complete fool of himself...
...distorting the stated aims and viewpoints and policies of the Republican Party.

So is Hillary the beneficiary of all this, or is she one of the reasons someone like Trump can get this far?
Hillary is part of the system. Bill Clinton famously...

...did not have sex with that woman...
...served two terms as president and served five terms as governor of Arkansas so the Clintons been around Washington for...

...whatever they could get...
...for quite a long time.

Isn't this one of the reasons Barack Obama beat Hillary for the Democratic nomination?
It is and a lot of Americans are sick of Washington. This is why so many of them have got behind...

...a tax cheat...
...a man with a business background, who's done it all. He started with nothing more than...

...$200 million...
...a few million dollars and he's turned that into...

...a haircut...
...He's turned that into a property empire and a lot of people admire that because whether they realise it or not he's a...

...a complete parasite...
...he's an example of the great American dream.

Do you think he can win?
In a two-horse race, you've got to think either one of them can win.

Well, thank you very much. It's been a...
...circus. It's been a complete circus so far...

...It's been a pleasure to talk to you and I hope the election...
...is postponed. Or cancelled. I hope they don't have it.

...I hope it goes well and thanks for your time.

The Hon. Scott Morrison
Treasurer of Australia

The market is the determining factor.

Scott Morrison, thanks for your time.
Pleasure.

The Reserve Bank left interest rates on hold this month.
That's right. We still have some concerns about a two-speed economy and until we have some greater uniformity about growth and exactly where its occurring, it's probably best to keep the settings as they are.

Have we got growth?
We've got growth in some areas of the economy.

In the Sydney housing market?
Not just there.

Where else have we got growth?
In the Melbourne housing market.

Why is the eastern states housing market having this sustained boom?
Interest rates are low; money is available.

Isn't there a better use of investment money than domestic housing?
What do you mean, a better investment? They're making a poultice, these people. They're cleaning up.

Better in the sense that housing doesn't produce anything.
It's producing jobs. That's why we can't put interest rates up. It's the only thing propping up the employment market.

Does it produce export income?
Yes, there's a lot of foreign money flowing into the country for Australian assets.

But isn't this like the mining boom? It works for a while and then it falls over?
What we have in Australia is a market economy. The market is the determining factor.

So why control interest rates?
Interest rates and fiscal policy are tools available to the government to ensure that things run even better.

The other thing that comes out of recent data is that the nature of employment is changing.
Yes, there's an increase in the amount of part-time work, right across the economy.

Yes, even happening at the prime-minister level.
No. Prime minister is a full-time position.

Really? So how does it work? Is it a job-share arrangement then?
No, Malcolm Turnbull is the prime minister. That's his full-time job.

So why isn't he running the country?
He is. That's what he does.

Malcolm Turnbull's running the country?
Yes.

So what's Tony Abbott doing?
Tony's not even in the cabinet.

This is what gives him the time, I suppose.
Gives him the time to do what?

To run the country.
Tony Abbott's not running the country. The job of prime minister is a full-time position and that position is filled by Malcolm Turnbull.

I accept that. What I'm asking is, who's actually doing the job?
Malcolm Turnbull is. He's the prime minister.

OK. So Tony Abbott writes the policy, and Malcolm Turnbull announces it.
Tony Abbott doesn't write the government's policy.

So why is the government's policy exactly what Tony Abbott wants it to be?
That's a coincidence. But you'd expect members of the government to be in agreement with government policy.

Presumably there are members of the government who disagree with aspects of government policy.
I can only think of one.

Who is it?
I don't want to be drawn into who that might be.

Why not?
It could lose him his job. He's got a full-time job. I don't want to dob him in. He's got a family.

A Weather Forecaster

It's a slow-moving system.

Thank you for your time tonight.
Good to be with you.

What's the position with these weather systems right now? Cyclone Debbie has gone through.
It has. It's a slow-moving system so it's taken a while. It's now moving offshore again although we still have some very high winds associated with that…

And a lot of damage…
A lot of damage, 200-kilometre-per-hour winds, a lot of debris. It's going to take a long time to clean up.

And a lot of the power was out.
That's right. Infrastructure was hammered.

And a lot of rain.
The rain was biblical. Still is, in some of the affected areas.

We're dealing with several weather systems at the same time here in Australia, aren't we?
We are. Not unusual. Other parts of Australia face weather systems that are due to make landfall in coming days and people in those areas will need to box a bit clever to stay out of trouble.

Are people being advised to stay inside?
They will be if some of these weather systems strengthen, yes.

It's a wait-and-see situation with these other systems at the moment?
Yes. We don't know quite what's going to happen.

Let's go through these other systems we've got. Did Cyclone Cory develop?
No. Cyclone Cory's been downgraded to a light zephyr.

I see here that Cyclone Bill is forming again.
Cyclone Bill has actually blown out to sea and looks as if it might
dissipate and become just a tropical low.

What about Cyclone Malcolm? Has that formed yet?
No. We don't know what's going on with Malcolm.

It's moving south, isn't it?
It's a long way further south than it was and it seems to have weakened
and combined with a lot of other smaller low-pressure systems. It's
moved back off the coast and doesn't seem to know what it's doing.

Wasn't some of the energy in Malcolm lost to Hurricane Pauline?
Yes, although a lot of the energy in Pauline was then lost due to
associated pressure coming from a severe thunderstorm.

Did the thunderstorm have a name?
Barrie.

And how do they measure the pressure in a thunderstorm?
Barometric pressure, which is sometimes a function of the temperature
in the sea, and that produces warm air.

What does that mean for Malcolm?
That means Malcolm could be on the move again. We just don't know.

Should people be worried by Malcolm?
Yes, they should. There's a lot of energy in a cyclone even if it's just
going around in circles and doesn't seem to know what it's doing.

Which areas are in danger if it crosses the coast?
If it hits with any force the towns of Dutton and Abbott could be in
trouble.

And what industries will be affected?
The loathing industry is very big in that area.

They do a lot of loathing in Dutton?
They do. And there's a lot of seething done not just in Abbott but through this whole area.

Just for anyone watching in Dutton and Abbott, should they leave now?
Yes, if you know anyone in Dutton, get hold of them and see if they require help.

Should they get out?
I'd get them out of there now, yes.

What about in Abbott?
Abbott's in lockdown now. There's a siege there. There's some guy there holed up, I believe, in an antique shop. They believe he's armed and should not be approached under any circumstances.

Even now?
Especially in these conditions, Bryan. Our priority is to keep people safe.

Thanks for your time.

An Energy Consultant

The watts were pretty much the same.

You're a consultant in the energy market.
Yes, I am.

We have a crisis in energy, don't we? The prime minister's been waving a yellow card all week.
We face some problems with the energy market.

I thought we had gas and electricity running out our ears?
We do but we face some challenges with the energy market.

Tell me about the energy market.
The energy market is where you buy your energy, either at a spot price or in terms of some contractual arrangement with a supplier.

Didn't all the energy used to be owned by the Australian people?
Yes, we fixed that.

It was all owned by governments. It was built by governments.
Yes, but it was hopelessly inefficient so a lot of it was privatised.

Who said it was hopelessly inefficient?
The people who wanted to buy it.

And how did they sell that idea to the public who owned it?
It was going to mean a lower cost to consumers. There were now a lot more players in the market.

More electricity producers?
No. More billing companies, and of course this provided consumers with a great deal more choice.

Choice of what?
No, the watts were pretty much the same but there was a choice of who to buy them from.

And so who bought the infrastructure?
A lot of that is still government owned. In Victoria, for example.

Owned by the Victorian government?
No it's owned by the Singapore government and the Chinese government.

Why have prices have gone through the roof? What happened when they removed the carbon tax to lower prices?
What happened to prices?

Yes.
They doubled, but of course that only affects you if you're buying energy.

But isn't that what people are doing, in the market?
You can't buy it if it isn't there. And remember these outages are exacerbated by extreme weather events.

Wouldn't an extreme weather event be a fair test of the system?
Yes, we don't have an energy system.

We have an energy market?
That's right.

And what's gas got to do with it?
When demand goes out the top of the chart the regulator's job is to step in and generate extra power, using gas.

How do they do that?
They don't. They haven't got any gas.

We export billions of dollars' worth of gas.
Yes but that's exported. That goes offshore. We need some of that gas here.

They can get a better price for the gas by exporting it?
Yes. It's a market.

But surely it operates in terms of government policy?
Yes.

What's the government policy?
(The lights go out.) Hang on. Wait for the lights to come back on and ask me that one again.

The Hon. Malcolm Turnbull
Prime Minister of Australia

Have a glass of water, Bryan.

Malcolm Turnbull, thanks for your time.
Good to be with you, Bryan.

You're having a bit of a rough time in the polls, aren't you? I know they change all the time.
The polls are a bit confused. They've got the Labor Party ahead of us.

By ten points.
Yes, but I'm ahead of Bill Shorten as leader.

Perhaps you should join the Labor Party.
I disagree with practically everything the Labor Party thinks.

Yes. It'll be like running the Liberal Party.
Have a glass of water, Bryan.

Prime Minister, why is the government attacking renewable energy when it's a growing industry and a very successful industry?
We support the renewables industry and…

And it's going very well, the renewables market.
It is.

So what's the future for the renewables industry, do you think?
Publicly or privately?

Publicly.
As prime minister, do you mean?

Yes.
In Australia or at some sort of international renewables forum where we want to appear to be interested in ideas?

In Australia.
In Western Australia or in Sydney?

Anywhere.
Look, I'm trying to help you narrow this down a bit here, Bryan.

It's a simple question.
I think that's where you've gone wrong.

What's the answer?
From what perspective?

From the perspective of the planet. Presumably you believe in climate change.
Publicly or privately?

Publicly.
As prime minister, do you mean?

Yes.
Does the government believe in climate change?

Yes.
All the government or some of the government? We've got a few mouth-breathers who might have to repeat a year on some of this stuff.

Let's change the subject. Do you think Section 18c of the Racial Discrimination Act should be changed?
Do I think it should be changed?

Yes.
Publicly or privately?

Publicly.
As prime minister, do you mean?

Yes.
I think there are more important questions facing Australia.

What questions?
These other questions we've been discussing.

Thanks for your time.
A most stimulating discussion, Bryan. Well done.